THE SKIN DIVER'S BIBLE

THE SKIN DIVER'S BIBLE

BY OWEN LEE

DOUBLEDAY & COMPANY, INC., GARDEN CITY, NEW YORK

To
Paulette

Also by Owen Lee

The Complete Illustrated Guide to Snorkel and Deep Diving

ISBN: 0-385-03737-6
Library of Congress Catalog Card Number 67–11191
15   14   13   12   11   10

Chapters 8 and 9 have been taken from *The Complete Illustrated Guide to Snorkel and Deep Diving* by Owen Lee, Doubleday & Company, Inc., 1963

CONTENTS

ACKNOWLEDGMENTS

This book could not have been written without the generous assistance and cooperation of James Dugan and Captain Jacques-Yves Cousteau; Stan Russell, who took many of the photo illustrations; Al Tilman, Dave Woodford, Jack McKenney, and Chuck Petersen of the Underwater Explorer's Club in Freeport, Grand Bahama; Al Giddings and LeRoy French of the Bamboo Reef; Jim Auxier and Paul Tzimoulis of *Skin Diver* Magazine; Chuck Nicklin and Bill DeCourt of the San Diego Diving Locker; Chuck and Joyce Irwin, Jerry Greenberg, Bill and Betty Bowling, Bob Ritta, Dimitri Rebikoff, Eric Barr, K. C. Li, J. P. Nathan, J. S. Potter, Jr., Pablo Bush Romero, Dr. Joe McInnes, Dr. George Bond and Dr. Charles Aquadro, Teddy Tucker, Robert Stenuit, Marty Himmel, Ted Haner, André Galerne, John Houston, Lynn and Gray Poole, the Santa Catalina Divers Club, and of course my long-suffering editor, T. O'Conor Sloane III.

To each my heartfelt thanks and best wishes.

Owen Lee

INTRODUCTION

Compressed-air scuba diving equipment remains today, as it has always been, the means by which divers can achieve the simple end of safely entering and leaving the underwater world. Within the physiological limits of compressed-air breathing, it has filled and continues to fill the requirements of the modern diver with admirable efficiency. Therefore, basic air scuba equipment has changed very little since its debut a little more than a decade ago. The sea has many faces, however, and her fascination is ever changing. Thus the diver's reason for diving is constantly changing as he discovers one new facet after the other. If he continues diving, one facet or another eventually captures his curiosity, and his interest in it begins to evolve. So does his knowledge and skill in dealing with it. Thus, the person whose primary motive in diving was simple curiosity might evolve into a knowledgeable expert in ichthyology, submarine geology, underwater photography, or salvage and repair. His library continues to grow, not with books about the sea in general, but with books on his special field of interest. His purpose in diving becomes the investigation of one or two special facets while his interest in other facets becomes purely cursory or even passive.

The purpose of this book is not to provide you with a reason for diving. It is only to provide you with the means of making that exciting discovery for yourself—that is, a fundamental knowledge of the tools and techniques of getting safely to and from the underwater domain. Once you master these, your end in diving will manifest itself quite spontaneously. And so, for the time being at least, the discovery of your personal end in diving must be considered the "end" in itself.

If you have gone beyond this stage in the experience of diving, you might wish to read my more comprehensive book, entitled *The Complete Illustrated Guide to Snorkel and Deep Diving* (Doubleday & Company, 1963), in which I cover in detail the most appealing of the many fields of special interest. These include underwater photography, spearfishing, wreck exploring, search and rescue, gold diving, treasure diving, salvage, and other fascinating aspects of diving. Perhaps that book will provide you with the more advanced knowledge you are now after. Beyond that, you are on your own.

Good luck and good diving!

Owen Lee

The rewards of skin diving are many.

Chapter 1

SO YOU WANT TO BE A DIVER?

Well, you have lots of company, and small wonder! The sea is the world's last and largest frontier. It covers 71 percent of our earth's surface and, to the modern underwater explorer, opens up a whole new concept of enchantment and beauty and endless opportunity. Already there are over nine million skin divers throughout the world from all walks of life; skin diving has even reached the point where some of the best diving areas are becoming crowded, like all other places of fun and pleasure.

After addressing a skin diving group in Boston not long ago, the local divers took me diving around an underwater mountain right in the middle of Boston Harbor. For those cold and murky latitudes the diving was fabulous. In fact, it was so pleasant that I used a full tank of air and returned for another. About the time I pulled the reserve on my second air tank, however, I noticed something rather peculiar at the base of this underwater mountain that caught my attention. It was perfectly rectangular and white—two very unlikely characteristics for anything seen underwater. I used my last bit of air to go down and see what it was. It turned out to be a sign: GET YOUR AIR TANKS RECHARGED AT NEW ENGLAND DIVERS SUPPLY INC.—24 HOUR SERVICE! At that point I realized that skin diving was here to stay.

WHY DIVE?

Of course, not all modern-day skin divers qualify as real pioneers, in the sense my former boss, Captain Cousteau, does, for example. Far too many go beneath the surface of the sea *to be discovered* rather than *to discover*. Many of them seek to prove their fearlessness by seeing how deep they can dive and so defy the laws of nature. Others want to find how many poor helpless fish they can skewer with their spear guns. One fashionable young man, it has been quipped, had just completed his aqualung training course. The first weekend after graduation he took his girlfriend out in his motorboat and anchored in water 280 feet deep. Knowing full well that the safe diving limit for a novice is about 130 feet, he nevertheless turned to his girlfriend and said, "Sweetheart, I am going to dive all the way to the bottom and bring up a handful of sand for you." She watched impassively as he donned his full array of equipment and rolled over the side. He turned bottom up and slid beneath the surface: 100 feet, 150 feet, 200 feet, 250 feet, 280 feet! Just as he reached the bottom, where he should never have been in the first place, what should he see but a beautiful girl. The diver was amazed by this lovely apparition, but the girl's lack of diving equipment bothered him. He could not

Your scuba is your passport to the underwater world. Photo Mike Church

speak with the air hose stuck in his mouth, however, and so he wrote on the handy plastic writing slate strapped around his wrist: "What are you doing so deep without equipment on?" The stranger read the note, picked up the crayon, and scribbled out her answer: "Stupid, I'm drowning!"

There are risks involved in skin diving, as in every sport. The element of risk alone is what attracts some people into skin diving—but they are invariably immature. They may even harbor a subconscious desire to end it all. On one of my speaking tours, I encountered a diving organization in Orlando, Florida, known as the Forty Fathom Club. One of the entrance requirements was a compressed-air dive to forty fathoms, or 240 feet—far beyond the depth at which nitrogen narcosis overcomes the diver. I tried to discourage this foolhardy defiance of the physiological laws of nature that govern man underwater, but the Forty Fathom Club went blindly on its tragic course. The inevitable result was a number of needless deaths and the outlawing of skin diving in several counties of Florida. If you are avid for danger, please don't become a skin diver, because you'll only give diving a bad name and impose restrictions on those who would like to continue enjoying the sport.

On the other hand, if you are a normal, healthy person who enjoys adventure and wants to live life to its fullest, skin diving is definitely for you. Indeed, if exercised with all necessary precautions, diving can be one of the most rewarding and thrilling experiences of your lifetime and certainly no more dangerous than driving a car. But to exercise sanity in skin diving, you must know what the precautions are and why they exist. You must know what to do and what not to do, and why. That is the purpose of this book. If you follow the simple instructions in this book and the guidance of a competent instructor, you can explore safely the last and most exciting frontier left on earth.

REWARDS OF DIVING

Once you learn the simple ABCs of diving, the fascination of the underwater world will grow with each new dive; you will find new things that capture your interest and imagination. You will no longer be content with diving as an end in itself but will find that it is only a means to greater ends. Without realizing it, you will develop certain underwater skills. You may become a spearfisherman or collect specimens for a salt-water aquarium. You may begin taking pictures to capture some of the enchantment and beauty of the underwater world on film. As a result of collecting bottom specimens, you may become interested in the geological aspects of the underwater world. You might find ways to use your diving skills in repairing boats or recovering lost items from the bottom of the sea. Or you may become a treasure diver and

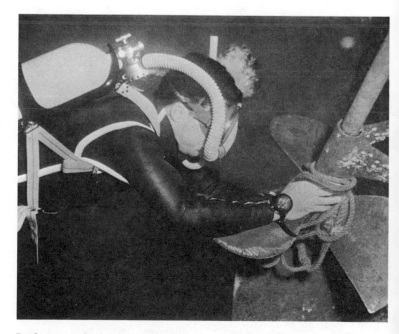

Scuba can be your entrée to a new profession. Photo Paul Tzimoulis

Scuba can be enjoyed by all ages and both sexes, for it is something you can do at your own pace. Photo Les Requins Associés

seek a fortune in sunken gold. If your interests develop far enough, you may even turn professional and thus embark upon a brand-new future.

WHO CAN DIVE?

To say that everyone can learn and enjoy diving would be a gross exaggeration. Obviously you must possess certain physical, mental, and physiological qualifications. For example, if you were a chronic heart or respiratory patient, it would be unwise to take up diving, as it would if you happen to be a diabetic or psychotic, an epileptic or a tuberculosis victim. An illiterate person who cannot read or write would also be disqualified from diving because he could not study the physiological principles involved in diving. However, if you possess a mature, healthy body and mind and are endowed with a measure of swimming ability and common sense, there is no reason why you cannot learn to dive with the best of them, regardless of age, background, or athletic prowess. Theoretically you do not even have to know how to swim, although a fair swimming ability must be considered a prerequisite if only because it conditions you to be at ease in the water and gives you a certain amount of self-reliance should you ever experience an equipment failure. If you are a parent and a bit apprehensive about your children taking up diving as a sport, I suggest you set your mind at case and join them. Diving is something that every member of the family can participate in at his own pace. In fact, as you associate more with other divers, you will quickly learn that one of the most important earmarks of the experts is the ability to exert a minimum amount of effort when underwater. If you simply remember never to allow yourself to become out of breath when underwater, you are likely never to encounter any difficulty. As you learn and practice diving, constantly remind yourself to take it easy. You'll soon discover how amazingly easy it is. Nonexer-

tion is the primary rule of diving and the primary reason why almost everyone can enjoy it with equal facility.

HOW AND WHERE TO LEARN

Last but not least, even if this were the *best* book ever written on the subject, it would take more self-discipline than you are likely to possess to learn from it all you need to know about diving. Ask a professional instructor to help you to *apply* your new knowledge. The YMCA in your community is the

Plan a scuba-diving vacation. Certified scuba instruction is offered at many resort areas such as the famous Underwater Explorer's Club in Freeport, Grand Bahama (above). It is also available through your local YMCA or diving-specialty store.

best place to look, for all YMCA instructors are highly qualified in teaching techniques as well as in diving procedures. Also the local diving and sporting-goods shop can direct you to a competent instructor as well as provide the basic equipment. Seeking instruction from diver friends who are unqualified in the teaching of techniques is not recommended.

SUMMING UP

To sum up, here are the qualifications you should possess before you take the big plunge:

1. A sound, mature mind
2. A sound, mature body
3. A competent swimming ability
4. A competent instructor

Chapter 2

SNORKEL AND SCUBA DIVING EQUIPMENT

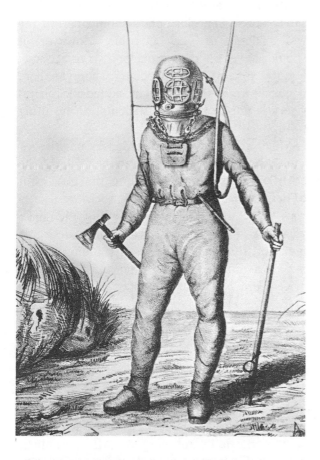

The early "hard hat" divers were limited in movement and remained tied to the atmosphere with air hoses. Courtesy Musée de la Marine, Paris

I like to divide diving into two categories: snorkel and scuba (self-contained underwater breathing apparatus). The basic equipment of the snorkel diver consists of a mask, snorkel, and fins or flippers. The basic equipment of the scuba diver consists of the snorkel equipment plus a compressed-air tank and a breathing regulator.

It is difficult to say which item in the basic equipment list is the most important, for without any one of them your efficiency in the water would be greatly impaired. Therefore each item should be given equal consideration. The first job of your instructor will be to familiarize you with this equipment. Pay close attention to his recommendations, and try the equipment out in the instruction pool before you invest in your own.

FACE MASK

Your face mask is your magic window to the sea. Without it, the water forming around the curvature of your eyeball creates an optical surface that distorts vision and focuses it somewhere behind the eyeball, as in a case of extreme astigmatism. The enchanting world beneath the sea becomes a ghostly place full of vague blurs and shadowy outlines. In the old days, pearl divers discovered that by placing a pane of transparent tortoise shell between the eye and the water, the shadowy outlines suddenly took on sharpness and definition, and so the divers devised a pair of goggles by setting panes of transparent tortoise shell in bone cups that fitted over the sockets of the eyes. Unless the panes were adjusted so as to be on the same geometrical plane, however, the divers saw double visions of everything and became dizzy and confused. They devised the single-plate face mask to allow both eyes to share the same vision through the same geometrical plane.

The modern face mask consists of a shatterproof-glass faceplate seated usually in a soft neoprene or rubber skirt and made watertight by a stainless metal band surrounding the edge. The skirt is flexible enough to conform to the contour of the face. Masks made out of material that is less pliable (such as plastic or hard rubber) should be avoided, for they usually allow some water to enter through smile and eye wrinkles on the face. Face masks whose *plates* are made of plastic or tinted glass should also be avoided. Plastic has a nasty habit of fogging and obscuring vision, and tinted glass diminishes the intensity of light that is transmitted to the eye. Light normally decreases in intensity the deeper the diver goes, and the diver needs all the light he can get.

Face mask with purge valve.

The mask should be an unencumbered piece of equipment, without any attachments or appendages. Masks that feature built-in snorkels are clumsy and dangerous. They are sure to give the beginner a good case of claustrophobia and might discourage him from skin diving forever. If you place the face mask in position and inhale slightly through your nose, the mask should stay in place without the help of the head strap. This is a good way to test your mask for proper fit or leaks before you buy. With the strap on, the mask should sit comfortably on your face without binding and without leaving red marks. The straps on most masks are adjustable, and a good fit can be accomplished with relative ease. The faceplate lens should be made of totally transparent, shatterproof tempered or safety glass. The glass plate should permit the widest angle of view possible. However, it should have no curvature or "wrap-around" feature, since distortion occurs wherever there is curvature in the lens. The added peripheral vision is not worth the disorientation resulting from the distortion.

Many masks feature molded-in cavities or squeezing devices that fit on either side of the nostrils and facilitate pinching the nose shut to help "clear the ears." Others feature a one-way valve that facilitates draining the mask of water. Both features are highly desirable but not essential. There are many diving masks available on the market, ranging in price from $2.50 to $18.00.

SNORKEL

The snorkel is a J-shaped tube made of plastic or hard rubber. One end is equipped with a soft-rubber bit that fits in your mouth, and the other end pokes into the air, allowing you to breathe air from the surface while your face is partially submerged. After inhaling, you exhale sharply through the same tube to blow out any accumulated water. However, try as you may, it is almost impossible to clear the snorkel tube completely of all water. The wise diver inhales very slowly, so that residual water remains in the snorkel, and he exhales sharply. With a little practice you will find this procedure becoming very easy and rhythmic, because no energy is wasted in raising your head out of the water for air. You can cruise on the surface for miles without becoming tired or winded.

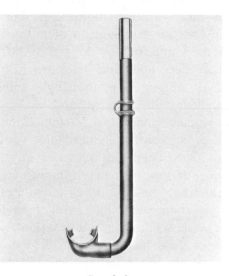

Snorkel.

A few snorkels come equipped with closure devices that fit on the open end. They usually consist of a ping-pong ball in a cage. Other snorkels are equipped with a purging valve that is supposed to keep the tube dry. However, it has been my experience that these contraptions never work properly and are more hindrance than help. The ideal snorkel is the simple J-shaped open-end tube, fitted with a soft-rubber mouthpiece that will not chafe the gums. The tube should not be longer than sixteen inches, for anything longer makes proper breathing extremely difficult. The diameter should be wide enough to allow the free passage of air adequate for your needs; the larger you are, the larger the diameter should be. If the diameter is *too* wide, however, you will find it difficult to clear the

snorkel of water. The rubber mouthpiece should fit comfortably between teeth and lips when the teeth are closed over the two small rubber bits. Simple J-type snorkels range in price from $1.00 to $2.50.

FINS (Flippers)

A fin or flipper can be described as a rubber shoe with a rubber paddle attached. A good pair of fins can increase your swimming efficiency as much as 60 percent, enabling you to move with the speed and agility of a fish while leaving your hands entirely free for useful work.

There are two general types of fins: The full-foot fin and the open-heel fin. The full-foot fin fits over the entire foot like a shoe and is superior to the open-heel fin that simply fits over the front of the foot and is held on by a heel strap. Because black-rubber products tend to hold up longer than rubber products with color pigment, and because fins should be as lively as possible, I recommend that you select black-rubber fins. The blades should be canted slightly downward for maximum thrust and should snap quickly back into place when bent.

Swimming with fins requires considerably more leg effort than swimming without them. Therefore, beginners should avoid the so-

Fins (Flippers).

called "giant fins" until they have developed their muscles to match the effort required.

It is extremely important that the fins fit the feet properly. If the fins are too small they will bind, bruise, and cause pain. On the other hand, if they are too large, you may lose them while swimming underwater. Try them on and, if possible, try them out before you buy. Prices range from $3.00 for the kiddies to $18.00 for the giants.

AIR TANKS

Although many pertinent research projects are currently under way, man has not yet devised a way of breathing underwater. In fact, the modern scuba diver never fully relinquishes his liaison with the surface atmosphere. He carries his atmosphere on his back inside a heavy steel cylinder containing air under pressure. In fact, the air pressure inside the tank is so great that the tank constitutes a potentially dangerous piece of equipment, and tanks are manufactured under strict regulations of the Interstate Commerce Commission. By law, the "pressure rating" of each air tank is stamped on its shoulder near the valve, together with the date of the last hydrostatic pressure test, the serial number, and the manufacturer's trademark.

It is a legal offense to charge an air tank beyond the pressure rating stamped on the shoulder, and with good reason. If a tank is charged far enough beyond its rated capacity, it can explode like a bomb. Furthermore, the strength of the steel cylinder weakens with time and use, because of corrosion and oxidation. The oxidation process is almost never discovered until it is too late, because it is concealed inside the tank. For this reason, the Interstate Commerce Commission further requires that all high-pressure air tanks be subjected to a hydrostatic pressure test every five years and receive a new pressure rating if required. Further, because of the weakening of metal through oxidation, it is wise to pur-

chase air tanks made of galvanized steel or coated with a protective layer of enamel inside and out.

Air tanks come in various sizes, capacities, and pressure ratings. The most popular is the one commonly called "the 71." It contains 71.2 cubic feet of air compressed to fit inside the tank at a pressure of 2250 pounds per square inch. The capacity is large enough to provide a man with at least fifty minutes of "down time" at thirty-three feet, but theoretically not large enough to allow a diver to go so deep and stay so long that he might contract decompression sickness or "the bends." It weighs 39 pounds, light enough to be handled with ease by most male divers. Some women prefer the 50-cubic-foot tank, which is somewhat lighter and yet holds enough air to permit an adequate stay on the bottom. For tiny women, beginning students, and children, the 18- or 24-cubic-foot tank contains enough air at 1800 pounds per square inch to facilitate instruction sessions and short stays on the bottom. The comfortable 26-pound maximum weight of these smaller tanks goes a long way to make up for the limited depth and time they allow underwater.

Air tank assembly.

Since all air tanks made for diving are manufactured to the strict specifications of the Interstate Commerce Commission, it makes little difference what brand name of tank you choose. They are all good. Therefore, it is best to select your tank on the basis of its weight, pressure rating, capacity, the type of air valve it has, the type of harness, the size of the neck opening, the protective finish, and the price.

TANK VALVE

Like a chain, the air tank is no stronger than its weakest link. The valve, which opens and closes the flow of air, must be able to withstand the pressure of the air inside the tank. Furthermore, the Interstate Commerce Commission requires all air valves to have a safety-release plug which will blow off at a pressure considerably lower than that at which the tank would explode.

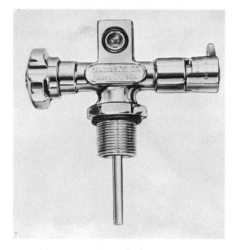

Air tank valve: J or constant-reserve valve.

Today only two kinds of air valves are commonly used with air tanks. They are the straight K valve and the constant-reserve J valve. The K valve is a simple open-and-close valve mechanism that provides air to the breathing regulator straight from the cylinder.

There is no built-in air-reserve mechanism. When the air pressure inside your cylinder becomes low, it gradually becomes harder for you to breathe. When at last the air pressure inside the cylinder becomes almost equal with the water pressure surrounding it, it becomes impossible to breathe. But the moment the diver begins his ascent toward the lesser pressures of the surface, the air in the tank expands and provides him with a few more breaths, which are adequate to get him safely to the surface. He cannot, however, go any deeper before starting his ascent. In fact, the only advantage of the K valve is the relatively small price of $8.00. Because of its lack of a constant-reserve device, I do not recommend it for depths beyond thirty feet.

If an air tank is equipped with a J valve, a spring-loaded shut-off device stops the air flow automatically when the air pressure drops to about 300 pounds per square inch. At that point the diver pulls a lever that releases the remaining 300 pounds per square inch of air pressure for breathing, and the diver knows that he has from five to fifteen minutes (depending on his depth) of air remaining in order to reach the surface. If necessary, he can swim deeper to free himself from entanglements or to leave the interior of a sunken wreck or a cave before heading toward the surface. The straight K valve does not permit going deeper once the air flow stops. Thus the J valve is highly recommended. Although it costs more than three times as much as the straight K valve, it is well worth the price.

HARNESS

A large variety of custom-made harness and back-pack assemblies are available to hold the air tank on your back. However, the assemblies that are sold with an air tank as standard equipment are usually the best. In any case, the harness and back-pack assembly should be made of material such as plastic,

Air tank harness and back-pack.

nylon, and stainless steel, which resist the corrosive and deteriorating effects of salt water. Make certain that your harness assembly includes a quick-release buckle so that you can easily ditch your gear should the occasion arise. If you acquire more than one tank in your diving locker, then it might be wise to consider one of the new clamp-on back-packs, which permit changing air tanks in only seconds. Back-pack and harness assemblies range in price from $15.00 to $35.00.

BREATHING REGULATORS

There are two radically different kinds of underwater breathing apparatus that fall under the all-inclusive term scuba. They are the compressed-air, open-circuit scuba and the closed-circuit, oxygen-rebreathing scuba. The closed-circuit, oxygen-rebreathing scuba is not available on the open market except in Army and Navy surplus stores, for it was designed primarily for military use. Since oxygen becomes toxic to the diver when breathed under pressures greater than those of one atmosphere (14.7 pounds per square inch; a depth of 33 feet is equal to one atmosphere) and requires constant adjustment, it is

potentially a very dangerous piece of equipment. Therefore, it should clearly be understood that whenever the term scuba is used in this book, it refers to the compressed-air, open-circuit rig and not to the oxygen rebreather.

The open-circuit, compressed-air scuba in popular use today was co-invented by Captain Jacques-Yves Cousteau and the French engineer Émile Gagnan in June 1943. Gagnan had developed several kinds of gas-flow demand regulators that were in common use on automobiles and in hospital operating rooms during World War II. Cousteau figured that with slight modification, these demand regulators could be used to provide underwater swimmers with air from a tank strapped to the back. Gagnan liked the idea and, after a few false starts, their experiments worked perfectly. In fact, the device was so simple, safe, and effective that it seemed to open the doors of the sea to intimate investigation for the first time in history. When Cousteau filmed and wrote about his experiences in the enchanting underwater world, thousands clamored for the chance to try it for themselves. Cousteau persuaded Gagnan's parent company, Air Liquid of France, to manufacture the breathing regulators for the consumer market, and thus the sport of scuba diving was born. The basic single-stage, dou-

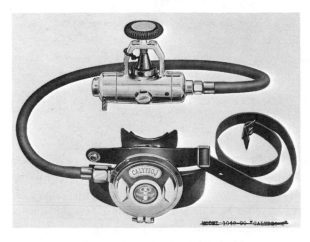

Single-hose scuba breathing regulator.

ble-hose regulator in common use today differs very little from the original prototype model that Cousteau and Gagnan first produced in France.

The single-stage scuba regulator consists of a noncorrosive housing divided into two chambers by a very flexible rubber diaphragm. On one side of the diaphragm is a watertight air chamber and on the other side a water chamber that is open to the sea. A corrugated rubber hose leads from the air chamber to the diver's mouth, and from his mouth it returns to the water chamber. Within the regulator, the air pressure on one side of the diaphragm is always equal to the pressure of the water on the other side. When the diver inhales he creates a slight vacuum in the air chamber. To fill this vacuum, the water must push against the flexible diaphragm, which in turn activates a lever that opens and closes a valve. The valve regulates the flow of air from the

air tank. When the diver's lungs are full, the vacuum ceases to exist, the water and air pressure are instantly equalized, and the diaphragm returns to its normal position. Thus it releases the pressure on the valve-actuating lever, and the valve closes. At this point, the

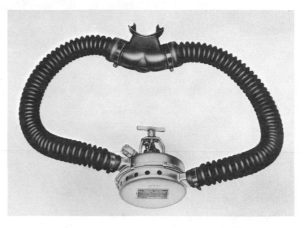

Double-hose scuba breathing regulator.

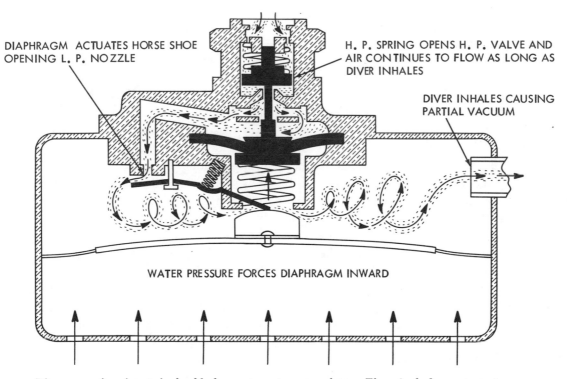

DIAPHRAGM ACTUATES HORSE SHOE OPENING L. P. NOZZLE

H. P. SPRING OPENS H. P. VALVE AND AIR CONTINUES TO FLOW AS LONG AS DIVER INHALES

DIVER INHALES CAUSING PARTIAL VACUUM

WATER PRESSURE FORCES DIAPHRAGM INWARD

Diagrammatic view of double-hose, two-stage regulator. The single-hose, two-stage regulator works on the same principle, but high-pressure (H. P.) stage attaches to tank valve while low-pressure (L. P.) stage is attached to mouthpiece.

*Author explains
popular single-hose,
two-stage regulator.*

pressure of the air inside the regulator air chamber (and inside the diver's lungs and throat and nasal passages as well) is in perfect balance with the pressure of the water that surrounds him, regardless of depth. For this reason, the diver is never aware of any squeeze from the pressure of the water. (The solid body tissues are of approximately the same density as water and are therefore virtually incompressible by water.) When the diver exhales, the exhausted air passes through the hose into the water chamber of the regulator via a nonreturn valve that keeps the water from entering. From there the exhalation rises to the surface in the form of bubbles.

The disadvantage of this kind of single-stage regulator (providing the diver with air directly from the tank) is that the air flow begins and stops rather abruptly. Engineers found that, if they first reduced the high-pressure tank air to approximately 100 pounds per square inch before it entered the regulator

air chamber, the abrupt start-and-stop of the air flow becomes almost imperceptible. Thus, the two-stage regulator was born. Later, they discovered that the bulky corrugated rubber hoses often created water resistance. Then they reasoned that by reducing the air pressure at the tank and fitting the second-stage diaphragm housing into the mouthpiece itself, they could provide the diver with air via a single hose of smaller diameter. Thus was born the two-stage, single-hose regulator.

Compressed-air breathing regulators vary in price from $27.00 to more than $100.00, depending largely on the materials used. Fortunately the difference in performance is not as great as the price range. Except for the cheapest models that employ a tilt valve, all of them work well regardless of depth and all of them provide the same fail-safe safety features that assure a constant supply of air. Should there ever be a mechanical failure, the regulator will never shut off the air supply abruptly.

On the contrary, the valve will remain open and provide a continuing supply of air that will not stop until the tank is empty. Therefore, the breathing regulator you select becomes largely a question of personal preference.

For the occasional sport diver who is unlikely to become involved in the arduous underwater labors that sometimes befall the professional, the moderately expensive single-stage regulators are quite adequate. Until recently, all my diving colleagues on Captain Cousteau's oceanographic expeditions aboard the *Calypso* used the single-stage, double-hose regulators. These range in price from $40.00 to $60.00. The more ambitious divers who expect to experience deep dives and strenuous effort might consider the more expensive two-stage models, which can deliver greater volumes of air at greater pressures. They are priced up to $120.00.

DIVING SUITS

Water is one of the most effective cooling agents known. About three thousand times more heat calories are required for warming a given amount of water than for warming the same amount of air to the same temperature. Furthermore, water tends to stratify itself into layers, according to temperature and density. These well-defined temperature layers are called thermoclines. The deeper you go, the colder they become, regardless of what the water temperatures are on the surface. When a diver becomes cold, the small blood capillaries near the surface of the skin open up, so that the blood can carry heat to the extremities. To produce this heat, the body burns greatly increased quantities of food and air to maintain metabolism. For this reason, the cold diver, whether he is holding his breath or breathing from a tank of compressed air, will increase his air consumption greatly. The diver who is cold will consume a tank of compressed air almost twice as fast as

one who is comfortably warm. Body warmth becomes not only a question of comfort in diving but a question of diving economy as well. If the body ever becomes so cold that shivering begins, then cold has become a health hazard, for shivering is simply the body's desperate attempt to produce heat by friction as a last resort.

There are two basic types of diving suits available to keep the diver warm: the "wet suit" and the "dry suit." However, it is such a costly process to manufacture a dry suit that really keeps the diver dry that most manufacturers have stopped making them. Those dry suits that are still made for the popular market are as ineffective as they ever were. We shall discuss only the "wet suit," the more effective, cheaper, and easier to maintain of the two suits.

Almost all wet suits are made of unicellular neoprene rubber about $\frac{3}{16}$ inch thick. Because neoprene rubber tears easily, the better wet suits also have a backing of synthetic non-deteriorating cloth such as stretch nylon for added strength. The properly tailored wet suit should fit skintight, but as the name wet suit implies, it does not keep the diver dry. A thin layer of water seeps inside the suit. For this reason, the water entry is always the most traumatic moment where comfort is concerned. But once the suit fills, the water is trapped there. It cannot circulate and carry off body heat, and the body very quickly warms the thin layer of water almost to body temperature. Thus insulated not only by the neoprene rubber but by the thin layer of body-warmed water as well, the diver can go in the coldest of waters in relative comfort. Because of the free passage of water the pressures inside and outside the wet suit are always the same. Therefore there are never any problems of suit squeeze with wet suits as there are with dry suits. The $\frac{1}{4}$-inch neoprene suits, being thicker, are slightly warmer than the $\frac{3}{16}$-inch varieties. Because of the required skintight fit, the wet suit should be equipped with

Dry suits.

Wet suits.

zippers at the arm, leg, and chest openings. Even then, entry is difficult unless you sprinkle the interior of the suit with talcum powder before donning it, so that the material will slide over the skin without binding or tearing.

Neoprene wet suits require a certain amount of postdive care. After each ocean dive, they should be rinsed thoroughly in fresh water and allowed to dry in the shade, because sunlight tends to deteriorate neoprene. Then they should be sprinkled liberally with talcum powder and stored in a cool, dark place. This preserves the rubber and keeps the suit in readiness for your next dive.

Ready-made wet suits are priced from $35.00 to $95.00, depending upon thickness and size. Wet suits come in many fancy colors and patterns; however, as I have said, color pigment tends to weaken rubber products, and I recommend that you stay with the standard black neoprene material. A few diving stores offer do-it-yourself suit kits at a considerably lower price.

WEIGHTS AND WEIGHT BELTS

Archimedes' Law states that "any object wholly or partly immersed in liquid is buoyed up by a force equal to the weight of the liquid it displaces." In other words, if an object placed in water weighs more than the water it displaces, it will sink and, conversely, if it weighs less than the water it displaces, it will float. If it weighs exactly the same as the water it displaces, it neither floats nor sinks but rather has neutral buoyancy. If the human body were all solid tissue, it would have neutral buoyancy, as body tissue is of about the same density and weight as water. However, because of the air cavities in the human body, such as lungs, throat, nasal passages, and sinuses, the body tends to float. A diver wishing to descend to the bottom could not do so without exerting an effort to propel him or without weights to counteract his natural buoyancy. If the diver happened to be wearing a neoprene wet suit, the suit itself might displace up to twenty pounds of water, depending upon its thickness. Therefore, the diver would have to carry twenty pounds of additional weight in order to counteract the buoyancy of the suit alone.

In the old days, pearl divers used to plunge to the bottom carrying huge stones so that they could reach their destination without effort. The modern diver wears a belt with a number of lead weights attached. By adding and subtracting the number of weights, he can adjust his buoyancy so that it is almost perfectly neutral; that is, he will tend to sink when he exhales and float when he inhales. He is able thereby to rise or sink with minimum effort. Because salt water is denser and therefore more buoyant than fresh water, the diver will need slightly more weights when diving in salt water.

All commercially produced weight belts are made of nondeteriorating synthetic fiber such as nylon. They are equipped with a quick-release safety buckle so that the weight can

Weights and weight belt.

be quickly and easily ditched in case of emergency. The weight belt should be worn over all other equipment so that it can be released without tampering with the other equipment in an emergency.

Commercially produced weights are almost always made of lead, which is the cheapest and heaviest material available. The standard-size weight units are one, two, three, and five pounds. A weight belt with quick-release buckle and weights will run from $5.00 to $20.00, depending on how much lead you'll require to sink. That depends on whether or not you wear a wet suit, which depends on the water temperatures, which depends on where you dive.

KNIVES

A sharp, sturdy diving knife is an indispensable safety aid, not a weapon. Only a fool

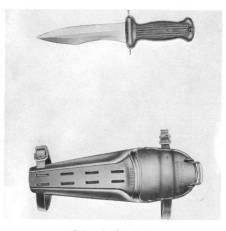

Diver's knife.

would pit his diving knife against a shark the way so many "Hollywood Divers" are depicted doing. A knife is a safety precaution against the possibility of becoming entangled in underwater lines or kelp. Since the knife is constantly exposed to the corrosive effects of salt water, it should be made of noncorrosive materials, such as plastic or rubber and stainless steel. In addition the blade should be fairly short, sturdy, and serrated on at least one edge to facilitate cutting fibrous material like rope. It should be kept handy at all times, worn on the belt or strapped to the calf of the leg. Good diving knives range in cost from $7.00 to $15.00.

PRESSURE GAUGES

If you take up scuba diving, you'll never know how much air your tank contains unless you have some sort of pressure gauge. If you don't know how much air your tank contains, you'll never know how deep you can dive or how long you can stay at any given depth. Furthermore, the pressure gauge is re-

Air-pressure gauge.

quired to carry out the predive and postdive check, all of which I will discuss later.

Basically, there are two kinds of pressure gauge: the permanent and the detachable. The permanent pressure gauge fits into a plug provided for that purpose on the air valve of the tank itself. Pressure is read simply the way a tire gauge reads the air pressure in your automobile tires. But remember, the diver wears his air tank on his back, and unless he has eyes in the back of his head, he finds it difficult to determine his own air supply while he is underwater. The underwater visible water gauge solves this problem. It is a dial gauge on the end of a long high-pressure hose that fits into the same plug. It gives the diver constant reading of the air pressure in his tank much as a clock tells the time of day. However, these gauges always seem to be dangling in the way, and because they are permanently attached to the tank, they are subject to many hard knocks. If you have a good constant-reserve J valve on your tank, the dial gauge is really not necessary, as the J valve itself is a kind of gauge. In addition to this the visible pressure gauges are rather expensive, about $24.00 each.

By far the best pressure gauge is the detachable one. The detachable dial pressure gauge clamps onto the mouthpiece of the air valve, just as the regulator does. You simply open the air valve, and the pressure registers on the gauge dial. The gauge itself is equipped with a breather valve that allows you to purge the gauge of residual high-pressure air before detaching it. This prevents the escaping air from blowing out the "O" ring seals in the valve. Testifying to its usefulness, almost every manufacturer of diving equipment has a detachable pressure gauge in his line. Most often used during the predive check, the gauge tells you how much air you have in your tank, and with that information you can compute how deep you can dive and how long you can stay at the bottom. The exact formula for doing this will be given in the Navy Decompression Tables in Chapter 8, explanation in Chapter 3. Prices of gauges range from $9.00 to $15.00.

DEPTH GAUGES

If you plan to use scuba gear beyond depths of thirty-three feet, you will also need a portable depth gauge to determine depth and the possible need for decompression stops. There are three basic kinds of depth gauge: the Bourdon tube gauge, the diaphragm gauge, and the bathometer gauge. Since water pressure increases at a constant rate (one atmosphere or 14.7 pounds per square inch for every thirty-three feet), all depth gauges measure depth in terms of water pressure. The Bourdon tube gauge measures the pressure by the tendency of a crescent-shaped tube to straighten out when subjected to water pressure. The diaphragm gauge measures the pressure by a hydrostatic principle. The bathometer gauge measures pressure by the compression of a column of air entrapped within the gauge by the water.

Navy depth gauge.

The depth gauge is worn on the wrist like a watch, and the pressures are calibrated on the dial faces in feet of depth. In each case the gauge is equipped with a small port through which water enters and leaves. Since salt water corrodes, it is important that the depth gauge be rinsed thoroughly in fresh water after each dive and that the entry port be kept free of salt and corrosion if you are to get accurate depth readings. Since the depth gauge helps to determine your depth-time limit and thereby your susceptibility to decompression sickness, it should be treated as the delicate instrument it is and not subjected to undue shock. The diaphragm depth gauge is the most accurate but the price makes it prohibitive in most cases. The Bourdon tube gauge is the most popular and sells for $6.00 to $15.00. The bathometer gauge is extremely simple, consisting solely of a sheet of plastic with a channel cut into it, and it sells for $2.00 to $3.00; it very seldom gives an accurate reading.

UNDERWATER COMPASSES

There is no sun, moon, or stars to guide you underwater. Sometimes, if the water is murky, it is difficult to tell which direction is up, much less which is north. A wrist compass is usually worn by divers who expect to have to navigate underwater. The compass rose card is usually suspended in a liquid-filled housing for easy visibility. The dial face should be as large as possible for it then makes for more accuracy and easier reading. The combination depth gauge and compass should be avoided, for it is a compromise instrument that gives compromise answers. Underwater wrist com-

Aqualung compass.

passes range in price from $3.00 to $30.00, and accuracy and price usually go hand in hand.

UNDERWATER WATCHES

The underwater wrist watch is an imposing instrument worn by many divers as a kind of badge. In addition to acting as a fraternal symbol, however, it is a very useful tool, both above and below the surface. Since all underwater watches are pressure proof, often to depths of several hundred feet, many people never take them off. In big, bold, luminous numbers they can tell you the time in the shower, tub, or dishpan, or at the bottom of the sea, night and day. Almost all underwater watches contain a movable time-elapsed recording bevel, which is used to record elapsed time and the duration of a dive. Handsome stainless-steel diving watches range in price from $25.00 to $250.00. A watch is a handy thing to have on, under, and away from the ocean.

Underwater wrist watch.

EMERGENCY FLOTATION GEAR

Preferring to believe himself capable of handling any situation, many a hairy-chested diver laughs at the mere idea of wearing emergency flotation gear. As for me, I consider it an essential part of my diving equipment. The chances are that you will never have occasion to use it. However, it is rather like the aviator's parachute. Should the need for it ever arise, you need it more than anything else in the world!

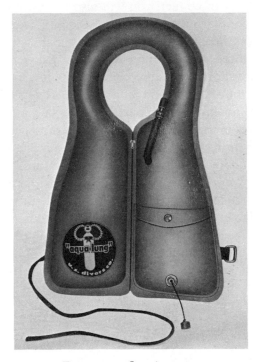

Emergency flotation vest.

Emergency flotation gear comes in several forms: vest, belt, package, even a new kind of inflatable suit. Most rely upon a small cartridge of compressed CO_2 to inflate some sort of flotation bladder made of rubber or rubberized fabric. None of them are very comfortable when inflated, but they serve the purpose for which they were designed, keeping you afloat, and very admirably at that. However, the pressure of the gas within the CO_2 cartridge is not enough to inflate a piece of bubble gum at depths of one hundred feet or more. They are useless for bringing you up to the surface except from the shallowest depths on account of Boyle's Law of Gases. You would not want to risk air embolism by such an uncontrolled ascent anyway.

Of the various types of floating gear, I strongly recommend the vest type, which has the tube for oral inflation as well as the CO_2 cartridge. This enables you to keep the vest inflated should it begin to leak and also facilitates adjusting your bouyancy trim while in the water—often an important consideration for swimming with heavy cameras or equipment on the surface for long distances. The vest type sells for about $16.00 and up.

PORTABLE DECOMPRESSION TABLES

As far as deep diving goes, knowing the time and depth will do you little good unless you have a copy of the U. S. Navy Standard Decompression Tables with you (see Chapter 8). These tables tell you the number and duration of the decompression stops you must make, if any, during your ascent to the surface. Leaving the Decompression Tables at home or in the car has cost some divers a serious case of the bends. Always carry a copy of the tables with you when diving beyond thirty-three feet. A few of the more advanced diving shops also offer the Decompression Tables silk-screened on a plastic card that can even be taken underwater. I repeat: Always take the Decompression Tables with you if you expect to dive beyond depths of thirty-three feet.

The Healthways Company has an automatic decompression meter on the market that simulates the reaction of the blood stream to compressed-air breathing and records the amount of time and depth of any decompression stops that may be necessary. It also considers the amount of interval surface time between dives if you are doing more than one in the same day. Though very accurate, it is a delicate instrument capable of error and should not be relied on to the exclusion of all else.

UNDERWATER FLASHLIGHTS

Most diving-equipment manufacturers offer an underwater flashlight that is pressure proof up to 250 feet. The flashlight comes in very handy when you are working in murky water, for invisible objects will often show up quite clearly when a source of light is held close by. The pressure-proof housings of most underwater flashlights are made of noncorrosive plastic or metal and come equipped with a plastic strap that can be worn around the wrist or attached to your belt. They range in price from $3.00 to $50.00, depending upon the materials. The Sealed Beam Dry Cell Units offered in most automotive supply stores also work well underwater and, in a pinch, an ordinary flashlight will give adequate vision for most jobs for a short period of time before the salt water robs the batteries of their power. After exposing the ordinary flashlight to salt water, you should remove the batteries immediately and wash the flashlight thoroughly in fresh water, otherwise it will corrode and become useless overnight.

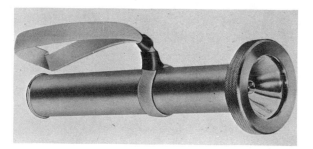

Underwater flashlight.

SELF-CONTAINED FLOATING HOOKAH

These gas-powered units provide air for two divers to depths of twenty-five feet via two plastic hoses. They are perfect for the occasional and weekend divers who like to go to

Aquanaut—self-contained floating hookah. Photo Evinrude Motors

out-of-the-way places where heavy air tanks are clumsy and air-filling stations inaccessible. You won't break any depth records, but who wants to? The most enchanting sights are in the first twenty-five feet of water anyway. The unit includes: float collar that can be inflated on the spot, Fiberglas housing for a two-horsepower gasoline engine and twin air compressors; two 25-foot lengths of vinyl hose and two full-face diver's masks. "Divers-down" flag is mounted to the engine's 33-inch exhaust stack of anodized aluminum. It operates from boatdeck or pier as well as in the water.

DIVING BOATS

Good diving boats are costly, but if you want to reach the best diving areas, they are almost indispensable. Anything from a pram to the *Queen Mary* will serve as a diving launch, and for the person of average income, the open-type skiff powered by an outboard motor can be perfectly adequate for all but the heaviest work in the open sea. Since it is a cardinal rule always to dive with a buddy, the boat must easily carry at least three men and all their equipment. It should measure sixteen to twenty-four feet in length, be of wide beam for stability, and be sturdily constructed of wood or, better yet, Fiberglas. It should have a wide, spacious cockpit with lots of deck space to hold the huge clutter of diving gear. The double- and triple-hull skiff known as the Boston whaler is ideal for such purposes, for it provides extra stability for entering and leaving the water. Ideally, diving

The double- and triple-hull-type boats are excellent for diving because of their stability in the water.

boats should be equipped with a glass panel in the floor so that you can inspect the bottom for good diving areas. A good sturdy boarding ladder is almost a necessity. If the water is murky or very deep in your area, an echo sounder is also a great aid for finding sunken reefs and wrecks as well as for measuring depth. Portable battery-driven echo sounders are available at prices from $110.00 to $250.00, depending on their power. Incidentally, an echo sounder can be encased in an underwater housing, just as a camera might, and used to measure horizontal as well as vertical distances.*

* The chapter "Search and Recovery" in my *Complete Illustrated Guide to Snorkel and Deep Diving* gives more information concerning underwater echo sounding.

UNDERWATER TRANSPORTATION

There are six types of underwater transportation available to the diver: tow sled, tow scooter, push scooter, aqua ped, wet submarine, and dry submarine. A diver can at least double his speed, distance, and the duration of his air supply by conserving energy through the use of any one of these.

The *tow sled,* sometimes called an aqua plane, is by far the cheapest and most practical mode of underwater transportation. It consists simply of a paravane with handles on it. It is towed behind the boat at the end of a long line. The diver holds onto the handles as the boat pulls the sled through the water.

Merely by pointing it upward or downward he can ascend or descend.

The tow sled can be used with either snorkel or aqualung. Its primary purpose is to facilitate underwater visual searches, and for this it is almost perfect. One big disadvantage of the tow sled is that the arms tire after the diver has been hanging on for a while, but this can be remedied by rigging up a harness between diver and sled with quick-release buckles.

Effective use of a tow sled requires a certain amount of practice and skill. One's rate of descent and ascent is much faster with a tow sled than without one. Therefore the diver runs the risk of popping an eardrum should he descend too quickly to clear his ears, or of incurring embolism should he ascend too quickly without purging his lungs of compressed air.

When you are searching with a tow sled, it is best to use a single-hose breathing regulator, for the double-hose regulators create turbulence and flutter violently as you are pulled through the water. If possible, you should rig an electric buzzer signal system between the tow sled and the boat operator. Boat operators tend to pull divers with tow sled too quickly, and any speed of more than three miles an hour is likely to tear the diver's face mask off. The tow line should measure three feet or more for every foot of depth that you expect to descend. Otherwise you have to fight to keep the sled on the bottom.

You can buy a tow sled ready-made for about $20.00 or make one yourself for half the price.

Electric-powered tow scooters are of either the push or pull type and are commercially available. They consist of a pressure-proof

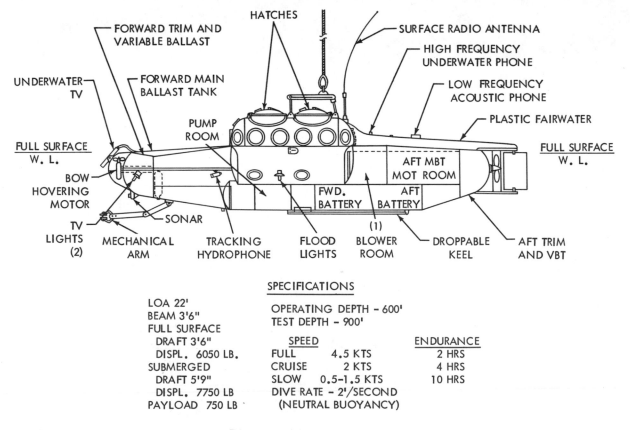

SPECIFICATIONS

LOA 22'		
BEAM 3'6"		
FULL SURFACE	OPERATING DEPTH – 600'	
DRAFT 3'6"	TEST DEPTH – 900'	
DISPL. 6050 LB.	SPEED	ENDURANCE
SUBMERGED	FULL 4.5 KTS	2 HRS
DRAFT 5'9"	CRUISE 2 KTS	4 HRS
DISPL. 7750 LB	SLOW 0.5–1.5 KTS	10 HRS
PAYLOAD 750 LB	DIVE RATE – 2'/SECOND	
	(NEUTRAL BUOYANCY)	

Diagram of Perry Cubmarine.

battery housing with a separate housing containing an electric motor that drives the propeller. In most cases the motor is activated by a hand pressure switch that stops the motor automatically when released. Most of the push-type electric motor scooters clamp onto the diver's air tank. The push-type scooter offers some advantages over the tow-type scooter because it leaves the diver's hand free for useful work and for protecting himself from underwater obstacles. Furthermore, there is no propeller wash in the diver's face as there is with the tow-type scooter. With the tow-type scooter the diver must hang on by two handles, much as with the tow sled.

The big disadvantage of most electric-powered scooters, whether tow or push type, is the maintenance. Most of them are underpowered and, unless the batteries have a full charge, are likely to go only half as fast and half as far as the manufacturers say they can. Electric-powered tow scooters range in price from $150.00 to more than $300.00. Because of the considerable investment required, it is best that you try before you buy.

The *aqua ped* is a kind of underwater monocycle that has two rather large counter-rotating propellers instead of a wheel. By pedaling as on a bicycle, the diver drives the propellers and is propelled through the water. It takes considerable skill and energy to work these with any degree of efficiency, and they are hardly worth the cost when compared to the simplicity and efficiency of the tow sled.

There are several kinds of *wet submarines* available to divers at various prices. Most of them consist of a Fiberglas hollow tube in which one or two divers may sit and thus acquire a certain amount of protection from the onrush of water. The submarine is towed

Perry Cubmarine in action.

through the water, much like the tow sled. It is equipped with two paravanes, one on either side, usually near the bow, which are controlled separately. As with the tow sled, you point them upward and up you go; if you point them downward, indeed down you go, and very rapidly at that. If you point them in opposite directions, you can do barrel rolls as if you were in an airplane. A few of the wet submarines can be fitted with a battery-powered electric propulsion system. However, as stated previously, these propulsion systems tend to be underpowered and we must await the invention of a reasonably priced battery that will deliver adequate power for prolonged periods. Wet tow submarines range in price from $250.00 to $500.00. They usually measure from ten to fifteen feet in length and weigh from fifty to one hundred pounds, depending upon the material used.

Dry submarines are available to the diver in several models. They range in price from $3000 to as much as half a million dollars and they can explore the depths anywhere from one hundred to one thousand feet. Obviously, most dry submarines are beyond the financial reach of the average diver. The Perry Cubmarine, for example, carries two men to a tested depth of 165 feet, is powered by a 4-horsepower D.C. electric motor, which drives a 15-inch-diameter propeller. The pressure hull is made of steel, and the outer hull is made of molded Fiberglas. The airplanelike controls are hydraulic, and, except for the propeller shaft, there are no moving parts going through the pressure hull. It cruises at a speed of 6 knots when submerged, and there are 12.7-inch plastic portholes through which passengers can view the underwater world to a depth of 230 feet. Available from Perry Submarine Builders, Inc., 2751 South Dixie, West Palm Beach, Florida, $26,500 up.

Chapter 3

THE PHYSIOLOGY OF DIVING

A COMPROMISING POSITION

Scientists are now experimenting to find ways by which men will be able to breathe water like a fish. If and when they achieve this goal, we will be able to remain submerged in the sea for unlimited periods. Meanwhile, however, we are chained to the atmosphere by the necessity for breathing. When we venture underwater, we must take our atmosphere with us. We must either hold our breath or carry tanks of compressed atmosphere on our backs. Either way, we place ourselves in a kind of compromise environment. Although we are living and functioning in the aquasphere, we are still dependent on the atmosphere. Accordingly we must make a number of psychological and physiological compromises in order to cope with it. For this reason, it is absolutely essential that we understand the limits and demands that will be imposed upon us.

AIR VERSUS WATER

The air that you breathe at sea level consists of 79.02 percent nitrogen (N_2), 20.94 percent oxygen (O_2), and .04 percent carbon dioxide (CO_2). Pure air is colorless, odorless, and tasteless, but it is by no means weightless. A column of air covering only one square inch at sea level and extending all the way to the outer limits of the earth's atmosphere (about seven miles) weighs 14.7 pounds. The same column covering a square foot at sea level would weigh 2,116.8 pounds. And if your body occupies an area of ten square feet, the column of air above you at sea level weighs 21,168 pounds! But don't get exhausted at the thought. You are not actually supporting such a tremendous load. You are simply living in it. Air is a mixture of gases, and, like all gases, its weight is transmitted equally in all directions in the form of pressure. Therefore, since the weight of our atmospheric air at sea level is 14.7 pounds per square inch, so the air pressure at sea level is 14.7 pounds per square

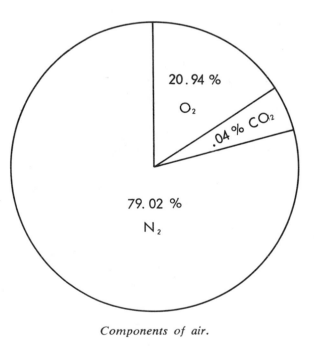

Components of air.

In arterial air embolism, air bubbles reach the brain via carotid arteries during ascent, blocking circulation and causing death or permanent damage if recompression treatment is not accomplished promptly.

Conjugal hemorrhage during descent ("face-mask squeeze").

Eustachian tube blockage prevents pressure equalization during descent, causing hemorrhage within the tympanic membrane and inner ear, and possibly eardrum rupture.

Blockage of sinus ostia causes painful aerosinusitis, with bloody transudate within the sinuses.

Cyanosis as a result of asphyxia.

Mediastinal and subcutaneous emphysema result during ascent when retained lung air expands, damaging pulmonary parenchyma. Less frequently, pneumothorax occurs from ruptured pleura.

Alveoli ruptured by expansion of trapped air during ascent allow air bubbles to enter extrapulmonary structures, including blood vessels.

You are always in a compromising position underwater because of the physiological effects of breathing gas under pressure. Courtesy of Spectrum, Charles Pfizer and Co.

inch. Since our planet is, for all practical purposes, spherical in shape and since seawater always seeks its own level, the weight and pressure of our atmospheric air remain constant all over the world. Thus it is used as a standard of measure by which we can express such things as heights, depths, and (by measuring the very slight changes in atmospheric pressure with a barometer) even the weather. Unlike air pressure, water pressure increases with depth at a very rapid but constant rate, so the atmospheric pressure at sea level provides an appropriate standard. You will often hear any kind of pressure measurement used in diving referred to in terms of so many atmospheres—that is, in units of 14.7 pounds per square inch (or 14.7 p.s.i., its abbreviated form).

When you leave the gaseous realm of our atmosphere and enter the liquid realm of our aquasphere, you enter a physiologically distinct world. Water is 800 times denser (thicker) than air. That is, the molecules in a given volume of water are 800 times more numerous and closer together than the gas molecules in air. Pure air weighs less than one-twelfth of a pound per cubic foot at sea level, the densest level of our atmosphere. Pure water (H_2O) weighs 62.4 pounds per cubic foot. A column of water only 33 feet deep weighs the same as a column of air of the same size that extends from sea level over seven miles to the outer limits of our atmosphere. Since the molecules of water are about as close together as they can get, and cannot be squeezed (compressed) closer together, unlike gas molecules, the weight of a given volume of water remains constant, regardless of how many volumes of water you stack on top of it. Thus you have the first example of how this atmospheric term of measure can be applied to the underwater world. Water increases *one atmosphere* (14.7 p.s.i.) in weight and pressure for every 33 feet of depth. Thus, a diver swimming at a depth of 33 feet could be said to be at a depth of one atmosphere.

GAUGE PRESSURE VS. ABSOLUTE PRESSURE

But is the diver actually swimming under the pressure of just one atmosphere of 33 feet of water or is he actually swimming under two atmospheres of pressure—that is, the pressure of one atmosphere (or 33 feet) of water *plus* one atmosphere (or the seven miles) of air above him? To be accurate in your measurements, you must differentiate between measurements of pressure by specifying *gauge pressure*—that is, the pressure of the water alone—or *absolute pressure*—that is, the total pressure of the water plus the pressure of the atmospheric air above the water as well. To facilitate this, all diving pressure gauges read zero (0) at sea level, and pressures are expressed as so many atmospheres or pounds per square inch *gauge* (p.s.i.g.) or so many atmospheres or pounds per square inch *absolute* (p.s.i.a.). Thus the diver swimming at a depth of 33 feet is under a pressure of one atmosphere gauge (14.7 p.s.i.g.) or under a pressure of two atmospheres absolute (14.7 p.s.i.g. plus 14.7 p.s.i. of the atmospheric pressure= 29.4 p.s.i.a.). However, since water increases at the constant rate of one atmosphere gauge (14.7 p.s.i.g.) for every 33 feet of depth, or .445 p.s.i. for every foot of depth, the same diver swimming at a depth of 66 feet would be exposed to a pressure of two atmospheres gauge (29.4 p.s.i.g.) and three atmospheres absolute (44.1 p.s.i.a.). At 99 feet the pressure would be three atmospheres gauge and four atmospheres absolute, at 132 feet the pressure would be four atmospheres gauge and five atmospheres absolute, and at 297 feet the pressure would be nine atmospheres gauge and ten atmospheres absolute, *ad infinitum*. Therefore, to find the pressure of the ambient (surrounding) water at any given depth, you need simply to multiply the number of feet of depth by .445. In order to find the absolute water pressure at any given depth, you simply add onto the above figure the pressure of the at-

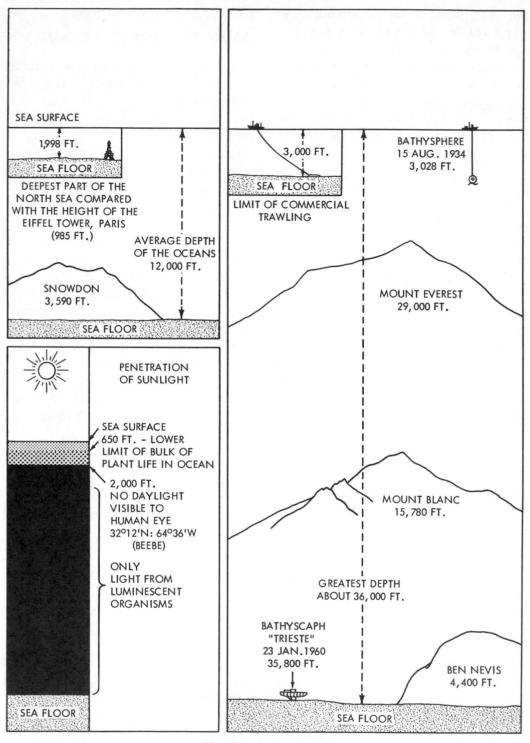

Depths of the ocean.

mospheric air at sea level (14.7 p.s.i.). Conversely, the depth in feet can be figured by dividing the gauge water pressure in p.s.i. by .445 p.s.i. Thus a depth gauge that reads zero on the surface at sea level is simply a pressure gauge with the last-stated formula (gauge) calibrated on its dial, in feet of depth.

BOYLE'S LAW OF GASES

The phenomenon of gas compression is expressed in Boyle's Law of Gases, which states that "at a constant temperature, the volume of a gas will vary inversely with the absolute pressure, while the density of a gas varies directly with the (gauge) pressure." In other words, if the pressure exerted on a given volume of gas is doubled, the gas is compressed to one-half its original volume but the density is doubled. It is essential that you understand this law of gases, for it governs the conditions that exist within the body when a man breathes compressible air while submerged in noncompressible water. To illustrate how Boyle's Law of Gases applies to diving, let us borrow a flexible rubber diaphragm from a friend and a quart glass cylindrical beaker from another friend and conduct an experiment.

Standing at sea level, let us seal the open end of the quart beaker (which is full of air

at 14.7 p.s.i.) with the rubber diaphragm and let us say that it now represents the lungs of a diver who is about to dive while holding his breath. If we invert the quart beaker so that the sealed end is down and plunge it 33 feet beneath the surface of the water, we note that the pressure of the water has pushed the flexible diaphragm halfway into the beaker. According to Boyle's Law, we can see that the original volume of air inside the quart beaker has been cut in half to one pint, and we surmise that the density has been doubled. If we plunge the beaker an additional 33 feet deep to a depth of 66 feet, we see that the volume of air is again cut in half to half a pint and we surmise that the density is again doubled. According to Boyle's Law of Gases, we know that this process would repeat itself for every 33 feet of depth. Now, if we withdraw the glass beaker to the surface of the water, we see that the reverse of this procedure takes place. The air inside the beaker expands until, once more at the surface, the air has assumed its original volume and the flexible rubber diaphragm has returned to its original shape.

Exactly the same phenomenon takes place inside the diver who dives to the bottom while holding his breath. Because the diver's lungs, rib cage, and diaphragm are flexible, like the

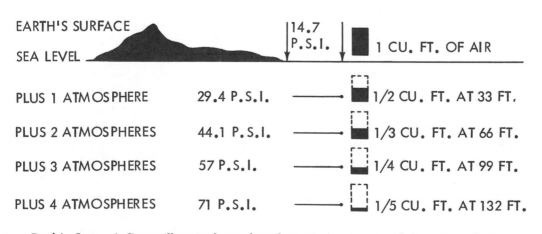

Boyle's Law of Gases illustrated, to show how air is compressed at various depths.

rubber diaphragm covering the open end of the glass beaker, the water pressure compresses the air volume inside his lungs (and other air cavities such as his throat sinuses and inner ears as well) to half of its original volume every 33 feet. When he returns to the surface the air expands until, once more on the surface, his lungs, rib cage, and diaphragm have resumed their original shape and volume. From the experiment above we see that there is always a balance between the air pressure inside the diver's air cavities with the ambient (surrounding) water pressure, thanks to the compressibility of the lungs and rib cage. (The diver's body tissues, such as muscle, bone, and skin, are of about the same density as water and are therefore incompressible by water. For this reason, only the relatively hollow air cavities are subject to "squeeze" by ambient water pressures.) We also see that for every change of air pressure within the diver's lungs and air cavities (resulting from a change in ambient pressure) there is a corresponding change of volume.

However, when a diver breathes from an aqualung tank full of compressed air, not only does the air pressure within his lungs and air cavities remain in constant balance with the ambient water pressure, but the volume of air within his lungs and air cavities remains constant as well. As explained in the chapter on aqualung equipment, when a diver inhales, he creates a slight vacuum that displaces a flexible rubber diaphragm separating the air chamber from the water chamber (which is exposed to ambient pressure) in his breathing regulator. As the diaphragm moves, it presses against a spring-loaded lever that opens a valve and permits high-pressure air from the tank to flow into the air chamber (and the diver's lungs). The flow continues until the air pressure on one side of the diaphragm is again equal to the water pressure on the other side. At this point, the diaphragm returns to its normal position, shutting off the air flow in the process. Then the diver exhales through a one-way valve and repeats the process with each new breathing cycle. Thus, thanks to the constant balance of air pressure and ambient pressure, his lungs are able to expand and contract to their normal volume, regardless of depth, and with such ease that he is hardly aware of the mechanism that makes it possible.

BOYLE'S LAW AND THE AQUALUNG

Now let us return to our original experiment to see how Boyle's Law of Gases applies to the diver breathing from an aqualung.

With the quart beaker still representing the lungs of a diver and still sealed and full of air from our first experiment, let us equip it with an imaginary aqualung and take it underwater to a depth of 33 feet again. Since the aqualung permits the pressure to increase in proportion to the ambient water pressure without affecting the volume, we notice that the flexible rubber diaphragm is not displaced at all but remains in its original position, regardless of depth. Thus, we know that the pressure both inside the beaker and outside the beaker is in perfect balance at 14.7 p.s.i.g. or 29.4 p.s.i.a. But now let us suppose that for some obscure reason the beaker (and the diver it represents) is suddenly deprived of its supply of compressed air from the aqualung. The diver's first instinct in such a case would be to hold what air he has in his lungs and return to the surface as quickly as possible. So, with the beaker full of compressed air equal to the ambient pressure of 33 feet firmly sealed (as the lungs of a diver holding his breath would be), let us withdraw the beaker quickly back to the surface and see what happens.

Since the ambient water pressure decreases .445 p.s.i. for every decreasing foot of depth, the air trapped inside the beaker expands and displaces the flexible rubber diaphragm proportionately. Since the ambient water pressure decreases 100 percent between 33 feet and the surface, it follows that the volume of air sealed inside the beaker doubles in the same distance. Thus on the surface we see that the rubber diaphragm bulges out.

But what about the poor diver whose lungs the beaker represents? The human lungs, when full of air, cannot be stretched more than 15 to 30 percent without bursting. Since a diver under threat of drowning can easily will himself to hold his breath, it is obvious that under such circumstances his lungs could burst like an overinflated balloon.

In such a case he would suffer what is known as *air embolism*. This is without doubt the worst thing that can possibly happen to a diver, for air embolism is almost always fatal unless recompression and medical aid are immediate. Therefore, it is most essential that you remember never to hold your breath during ascent while diving with compressed gas.

You should rehearse this fact in your mind so well that whenever you think of *ascent,* you automatically think to breathe normally while doing so. Even if you have the unlikely experience of being suddenly deprived of your air supply while on the bottom, you must purge your lungs of all compressed gas during ascent or you will run a grave risk of suffering air embolism.

When air embolism occurs, air bubbles are forced into the blood stream through the ruptured capillaries in the lungs. Any bubble too large to pass through constricted areas will form an "embolus" (blood clot) that obstructs the circulation of life-giving blood. And the dependent body tissues quickly die. If an embolus lodges in the brain, death or severe brain damage is sure to result within a few minutes.

In addition to air embolism, there are other

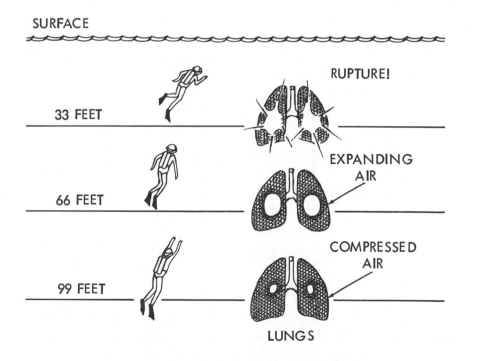

SURFACE

33 FEET — RUPTURE!

66 FEET — EXPANDING AIR

99 FEET — COMPRESSED AIR

LUNGS

DANGEROUS BREATH-HOLDING ASCENT
CAUSES COMPRESSED AIR IN SCUBA DIVER'S LUNGS TO EXPAND
AS WATER PRESSURE DECREASES. RUPTURE RESULTS.

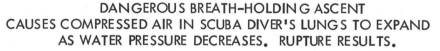

Effects of breath-holding in rapid ascent.

maladies that might result from failure to equalize the pressures inside and outside the lungs during ascent.

Mediastinal emphysema occurs when compressed air escapes from a ruptured lung and accumulates inside the chest cavity. The pressure of this air hampers the function of the vital organs such as the heart, blood vessels, esophagus.

Subcutaneous emphysema results when air from the ruptured lung lodges in the tissues beneath the skin, usually ballooning the skin around the neck and collarbone. It is usually associated with mediastinal emphysema.

Pneumothorax results when compressed air from a ruptured lung forms in a pocket between the lung covering and the chest wall. This air can hamper the function of the vital organs or even collapse the lung as it expands during ascent.

Although these last-described maladies alone are much less serious than true air embolism, they frequently accompany air embolism and are the only obvious signs and symptoms of its presence. Thus, with these as with air embolism, an ounce of prevention is worth almost all the possible cure you can muster.

Whenever you dive with compressed gas, *remember to:*

1. Exhale all the way to the surface during emergency ascents.
2. Breathe normally throughout all normal ascents.

OTHER APPLICATIONS OF BOYLE'S LAW

According to Boyle's Law, as we have seen, any air cavity such as the lungs whose interior air pressure is not in perfect balance with the ambient pressure is distorted in direct proportion to the pressure differential. But Boyle's Law does not apply to the lungs alone. Whenever the mask, diving suit, sinuses or any kind of semirigid mechanical apparatus or housing that depends upon a gas pressure to counter-

act the ambient water pressures fails to equalize, Boyle's Law comes into play. The ears, for example, are acutely affected by the slightest differential between the air pressure in the inner ear and the water pressure on the outer ear. Furthermore, because of their peculiar physical structure, you must learn a certain technique to "equalize" or "clear" them. All the other air cavities in the body "equalize" and vent themselves automatically as long as breathing remains normal.

The ears. The eardrum divides each ear into two parts, the inner ear and the outer ear. The eardrum is so sensitive to pressure differentials that sound waves are powerful enough to make it vibrate (otherwise you could not hear!). Any displacement of the eardrum greater than that caused by normal sound waves is likely to cause acute pain. Most people have experienced this descending for a landing in an airplane or descending from a mountaintop in a car. Thus, submerged in a liquid in which the pressure changes 100 percent in just 33 feet, your ears are severely affected by the pressure change resulting from any vertical movement.

Normally, the pain of pressure in the ears will prevent you from diving any deeper than from ten to fifteen feet beneath the surface unless you "clear your ears" or equalize the air pressure in your inner ear with the ambient water pressure. This is done by consciously snorting air into your inner ears via the Eustachian tubes—small, mucus-lined tubes connecting the nasal passages with the inner ears —until pressures inside and outside the eardrums are equal. If you were to continue your dive without "equalizing," the chances are that you would soon suffer hemorrhage within the tympanic membrane and inner ear and possibly eardrum rupture and sinus bleeding.

As mentioned previously, it requires a certain amount of technique and practice to be able to "equalize" or "clear" your ears. For the professional diver who is accustomed to it, working the jaws, wiggling the nose, swallow-

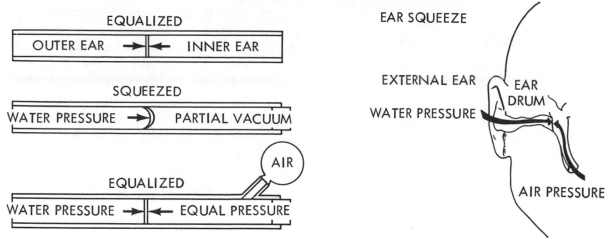

Effects of unequalized pressure on the ears and sinuses.

ing, yawning or chewing on the mouthpiece is usually enough to facilitate the equalizing process. If you are a beginner or an occasional diver, however, it is sometimes difficult. You must try to snort air through your nose while pinching off your nostrils to force the air through the Eustachian tubes. Many of the better face masks are molded with indentations that fit on either side of the nose or with some other nose-pinching device to facilitate "equalizing" or "clearing." You frequently must try several times before you succeed, and very often one ear will equalize while the other stubbornly refuses. When this occurs, ascending a few feet to relieve the pressure (which tends to squeeze the Eustachian tube shut) and then trying again will often help. If you are suffering from hay fever or a head cold, the Eustachian tubes (along with other mucus membranes) become irritated, swollen, and obstructed with mucus, thus preventing equalization. In such cases it is best to refrain from diving until the condition is relieved. In any case, "equalizing" or "clearing" your ears must be considered one of the basic skills required in diving, and the chances are that you won't enjoy diving until you learn to do it with

ease. However, practicing at home can be dangerous, for if you snort too forcefully, you can blow out an eardrum.

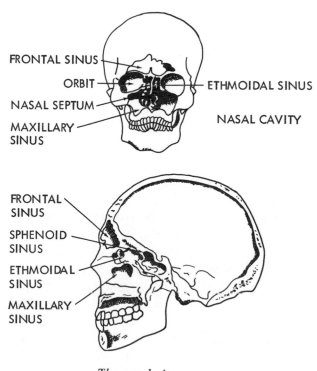

The nasal sinuses.

HYPERVENTILATION

If you are a normal person, the billions of tiny cells in your body are continually combining food calories with oxygen and burning them up by a chemical oxidation process called metabolism. This combustion process gives off a waste material comprised of carbon dioxide, water and heat. If any body cell is deprived of its share of fuel, the fires in its furnace slowly die. Also, if the exchange of fuel for waste does not take place at the same rate, the cell becomes suffocated. It is clear, therefore, that metabolism requires several exchanges of gases during each breathing cycle: first, between the blood and the oxygen in the lungs; second, between the oxygen-carrying blood and the tissue fluids; third, between the tissue fluids and the cells. The procedure is then reversed. The cells exchange oxygen for wastes (including CO_2). The waste gases are returned to the lungs by the blood stream, and the lungs exhale the waste gases. With inhalation the cycle begins again.

When the diver holds his breath, his body cells do not drop dead like proverbial flies. They continue to burn the residual oxygen in the blood stream. The exchange continues but not without a build-up of waste content (CO_2) within the blood stream. When you pant after holding your breath, it is just nature's way of purging your blood stream of excess wastes. What happens is this: inside the main arteries, tiny censors called chemoreceptors monitor the oxygen content of the blood stream. When the oxygen content gets too low or the waste CO_2 content gets too high, chemoreceptors send impulses to the respiratory center in the brain to increase the breathing rate. This involuntary urge to breathe drives every snorkel diver back toward the surface for air.

By supersaturating the blood stream with oxygen, the diver can greatly increase the amount of time before this urge to breathe occurs. This is done by hyperventilation: repeatedly inflating and deflating the lungs to the fullest extent for periods of from one to three minutes before diving. Purging the blood stream of carbon dioxide (CO_2) waste accompanies this procedure. Thus the diver beginning his dive under almost ideal physiological circumstances can easily double his breath-holding time.

SHALLOW-WATER BLACKOUT

Hyperventilation is used by almost all champion snorkel divers and spearfishermen. However, it has probably caused more diving deaths than all other factors combined, for a diver can consciously repress the urge to breathe until he is overcome with oxygen starvation or anoxia. After the diver represses the first few urges delivered by the chemoreceptors, the urge to breathe seems to subside. This is obviously a very dangerous point. The diver can lose consciousness in what is known as "shallow-water blackout" and not remember anything when he is by chance revived by artificial respiration. Thus, such competitions as breath-holding contests should be avoided at all costs. There have been several recorded incidents in which divers have continued swimming underwater even after blacking out, and so it is difficult to detect for both practitioner and observer.

Another fact to remember when hyperventilating is that the deeper you dive, the longer you can stay at the bottom. When you are on the bottom the ambient water pressures compress the air in your lungs according to Boyle's Law. The blood stream finds it easier to absorb oxygen from compressed air than from air at normal sea level pressures. Thus you are able to consume almost the total amount of oxygen in your lungs before having to "break for the surface." When at last you do ascend, however, the air in your lungs expands and the partial pressure of the oxygen in your lungs—already low—decreases sharply. Thus it is theoretically possible to starve yourself of oxygen to the point of "blacking out" during the ascent, even though you feel no discomfort while at the bottom. In addition, any excess of carbon dioxide in the blood stream is extremely taxing on the cardiovascular system, especially when combined with great exertion. When consistently repeated, excessive breath-holding like that done by professional spear-fishermen, for example, has even been known to cause some brain damage, which causes some divers to act slightly punch-drunk. But carbon dioxide (shallow-water) blackout and oxygen starvation are not limited to the breath-holding snorkel divers. So let us now consider how they affect the compressed air scuba diver.

DALTON'S LAW OF PARTIAL PRESSURES

Dalton's Law of Partial Pressures states: "The total pressure exerted by mixture of gases is the sum of the pressures that would be exerted by each of the gases if it alone were present and occupied the total volume." Thus, air containing only 2 percent carbon dioxide by volume at 132 feet or 5 atmospheres absolute has the same partial pressure of CO_2 and produces the same results (that is, blackout or loss of consciousness) as air at sea level containing as much as 10 percent carbon dioxide.

CARBON MONOXIDE (CO) POISONING

Exposure to only slight amounts of carbon monoxide (CO) can also cause blackout, anoxia, and oxygen starvation, although by an entirely different physiological process from that described above. The red corpuscles of the blood and the tissues they serve absorb carbon monoxide almost two hundred times more rapidly than they absorb oxygen. Therefore, any carbon monoxide in the air you breathe will quickly supersaturate the red corpuscles of the blood and render them incapable of absorbing anything else, including oxygen. Thus, body tissues are deprived of the oxygen on which they depend for life and soon die.

Carbon monoxide poisoning can cause unconsciousness with little or no warning. However, carbon monoxide is not a normal component of air. It results only from fuel combustion, and the only way it can contaminate your air supply is through the air compressor used to charge your air tanks. Therefore, the air intake of all air compressors used to compress air for breathing should be placed well away and upwind from the exhausts of all internal combustion engines, including its own. Ideally the compressor itself should be lubricated with some nonpetroleum products such as soap and water or vegetable oil. If you buy your air from a commercial air-filling station, be sure its air has been inspected and certified pure.

NITROGEN NARCOSIS: RAPTURE OF THE DEPTHS

The partial pressure of nitrogen in the air that you breathe imposes limits on the depths to which you can dive safely. When breathed under pressure, the normal amount of nitrogen in the air induces a narcotic effect on the diver that deprives him of his senses and renders him incapable of logical reasoning. This phenomenon is called narcosis or "rapture of the depths." It begins at a depth somewhere around 130 feet and gets worse the deeper you go and the longer you stay. The effect is the same as getting sloppy drunk on alcohol. Some people want to cry, some people want to laugh. It depends upon the individual. In each case the person is robbed of his good judgment. He is indeed drunk with the depths, and the simplest task can become more than he can cope with. I once tied and untied an overhand knot at least a dozen times before I finally caught on to what was happening to me and struck out for the surface. On my return to the topside of the 130 foot mark where nitrogen narcosis begins, it vanished mysteriously and left no hangover. Sometimes the diver can, by sheer willpower and concentration, overcome nitrogen narcosis long enough to get a job done, but even then he can never be sure if and how he actually did the job. Obviously, under such conditions the diver becomes dangerous not only to himself but also to the people with whom he is working. Since the most interesting diving depths are this side of 130 feet where nitrogen narcosis begins anyhow, it is best to limit the depth of your dives to 130 feet. There is no other way of avoiding it so long as you are breathing compressed air.

Together with decompression sickness or "the bends," nitrogen narcosis is the greatest limiting factor of compressed-air diving. Within the Navy and sophisticated commercial diving organizations, compressed air has been replaced with exotic mixtures of various inert gases such as helium and oxygen. With the nitrogen removed, so is the threat of nitrogen narcosis. These exotic mixtures may allow men to dive to depths of as much as three thousand feet some day. Meanwhile, however, helium is rare and very costly, and its availability is controlled by our government. Deep diving on artificial atmosphere is far beyond the reach of the average diver.

HENRY'S LAW OF GASES

Henry's Law of Gases states that "the amount of gas that will dissolve in a liquid at a given temperature is almost directly proportional to the partial pressure of that gas." In other words, a liquid will tend to absorb the air (gas) to which it is exposed until the pressure of the air both within and without the liquid is equal. For example, the surface water of the sea is saturated with air at sea level pressure. Similarly, our blood stream is saturated with air at sea level pressure (or the pressure of whatever altitude you happen to live at), and the compressed air in the div-

er's blood stream tends to become saturated with the air that he breathes at the pressure of whatever depth he happens to be working at. If he is working at a depth of three atmospheres, or ninety-nine feet, his blood stream tends to become saturated with air at a pressure of three atmospheres. The same thing happens in reverse to pilots who fly into the lower pressures of the atmosphere. The blood stream of the test pilot who takes off from sea level and rockets through our atmosphere to the edge of space (where the absolute ambient pressure is zero) would tend to become desaturated with air at sea level pressure until there was no air left in his blood stream if he did not wear a pressure suit. But this process does not take place instantaneously. It requires nearly twelve hours to thoroughly saturate or desaturate a liquid.

You can see Henry's Law of Gases in action every time you open a bottle of soda pop. Before the soda water was sealed inside the pop bottle at the factory, it had been saturated with a gas (usually carbon dioxide) at a pressure of at least one to several atmospheres. So long as the bottle cap remains tightly sealed over the bottle, the pressure within the bottle —both inside and outside the liquid—remains the same, and no bubbles appear in the liquid. But when the bottle is uncapped, the liquid within is exposed to a very sudden drop in ambient pressure. The gas within the liquid and outside it immediately tends to equalize in pressure. That is, the liquid begins to give off its excess pressure of gas in the form of bubbles. And that's what gives your soda pop all its fizz and sparkle. (Since it takes twelve hours to thoroughly saturate or desaturate a liquid, the soda water will continue to give off some bubbles for twelve hours before it becomes thoroughly "flat.") If a diver whose blood stream had been saturated at a depth of from at least one to several atmospheres of pressure were to suddenly shoot to the surface, the effect of the sudden decrease in pressure would be identical to that which happened to

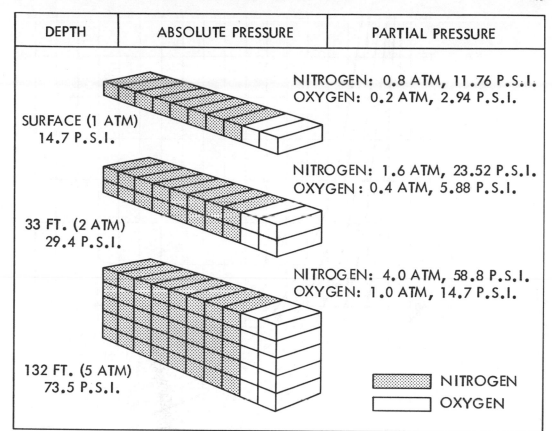

DEPTH	ABSOLUTE PRESSURE	PARTIAL PRESSURE
SURFACE (1 ATM) 14.7 P.S.I.		NITROGEN: 0.8 ATM, 11.76 P.S.I. OXYGEN: 0.2 ATM, 2.94 P.S.I.
33 FT. (2 ATM) 29.4 P.S.I.		NITROGEN: 1.6 ATM, 23.52 P.S.I. OXYGEN: 0.4 ATM, 5.88 P.S.I.
132 FT. (5 ATM) 73.5 P.S.I.		NITROGEN: 4.0 ATM, 58.8 P.S.I. OXYGEN: 1.0 ATM, 14.7 P.S.I.

NITROGEN
OXYGEN

the uncapped soda water. The air in his blood stream would immediately tend to equalize with the sudden drop in ambient pressure. As the gas came out of solution in his blood to rejoin the ambient atmosphere, bubbles would form. Blood corpuscles form clots around air bubbles. These clots usually lodge at constricted areas like joints of the limbs and generally pinch off and damage the nerves, resulting in paralysis. If they don't lodge there, they may travel to the brain where they can cause brain damage or even death. Thus, when you open a bottle of your favorite soda pop and watch the bubbles fizz, you are watching a case of decompression sickness (commonly known as the bends) take place before your very eyes.

However, if you were to cover with your thumb a freshly uncapped bottle of soda water, bubbling and fizzing for all it's worth, and take it underwater, you would not have to

Henry's Law in action.

dive very far before the soda water would stop fizzing and the bubbles would vanish, for the ambient pressures of the water would soon overcome that of the soda and the transfer of gas would soon be reversed. Likewise, if you were to send the stricken diver back underwater to a depth where the ambient pressure of the water would at least equal the

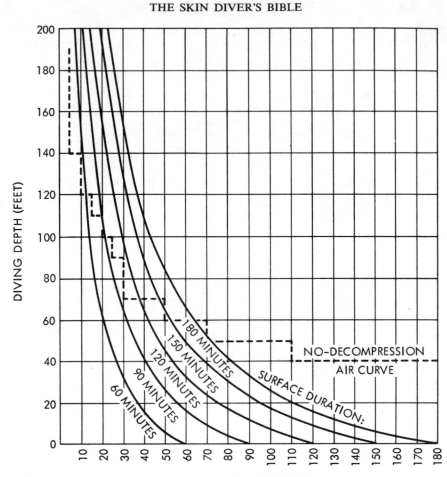

Depth-time ratio for compressed-air tanks at various depths for constant volumetric use (work) rates, giving surface durations indicated with relation to the no-decompression air-diving curve. Average air consumption at surface is about one cubic foot per minute (.9 CFM). Thus, standard 71.2-cubic-foot tank should last about seventy minutes at the surface, depending more or less on the individual's breathing habits and exertion.

pressure of the gas dissolved in his blood stream, the bubbles would vanish. As a result the blood clots would break up and no further nerve or tissue damage could be done. For this reason, if there is no decompression chamber convenient, a diver suffering the bends is sometimes sent back underwater at least as deep as he had been in the first place, or deeper. Then he is brought back to the surface very slowly according to a strict depth schedule known as the Decompression Tables, so that the pressure differential never becomes

so great that the gas comes out of solution before the lungs can pass it off. However, since the diver may have already suffered some irreparable nerve damage, he may not be in control of all his faculties. Therefore, whenever possible, equivalent measures are taken by placing him under pressure in the controlled environment of a recompression chamber.

However, recompression chambers are fairly rare, and much invaluable time is often lost in transporting the victim to the site,

Deep dives should be avoided unless recompression chamber like this one is handy.

during which irreparable damage can be done. Before making any decompression dives, it is best to learn the location and the quickest mode of transportation to all nearby recompression chambers. These can be found by calling your local U. S. Coast Guard or Naval Station.

DECOMPRESSION TABLES

The modern Decompression Tables for diving were born in 1907 when an English scientist, J. B. S. Haldane, discovered that a liquid could hold a gas in solution until its partial pressure amounted to about twice the ambient pressures. Therefore, according to Boyle's and Henry's Laws, a diver saturated with air at thirty-three feet could come all the way to the surface without stopping regardless of duration of the dive while a diver saturated at one hundred feet could come all

Portable recompression chamber in use. Photo International Underwater Contractors

LENGTH OF TIME SCUBA DIVER MAY REMAIN
SUBMERGED IN RELATION TO WATER DEPTH

DEPTH IN FEET	ONE CYLINDER IN MINUTES	TWO CYLINDERS IN MINUTES
0 SURFACE	100	200
33	50	100
66	33	66
99	25	50
132	20	40
165	16	33
198	14	28
231	12	25
264	11	22
297	10	20

DEPTH & TIME LIMITS – NO DECOMPRESSION
MAXIMUM SAFE RATE OF ASCENT = 60 FEET PER MIN. (1 FT/SEC)

DEPTH	TIME
0 TO 33 FEET	UNLIMITED
35 FT.	310 MINUTES
40 "	200 "
50 "	100 "
60 "	60 "
70 "	50 "
80 "	40 "
90 "	30 "
100 "	25 "

TOTAL DIVING TIME IN MINUTES
BASED ON STANDARD SINGLE 70-CUBIC-FOOT TANK

DEPTH	TIME
0	90 MIN.
10 FT.	69 "
20 "	56 "
30 "	47 "
40 "	41 "
50 "	36 "
60 "	32 "
70 "	29 "
80 "	26 "
90 "	25 "
100 "	25 "

No-decompression limits.

the way up to thirty-three feet without stopping regardless of the duration of the dive. From these findings, scientists who were concerned with diving and caisson work were able to compute the depths and duration of "decompression stops" that would enable a diver to return to the surface in stages without the threat of decompression sickness. These findings were reconfirmed by the U. S. Navy Experimental Diving Unit and the U. S. Navy Medical Research Laboratory in New London, Connecticut. The U. S. Navy Standard Air Decompression Tables are a result of these efforts (see Chapter 8). They have been tested and retested by thousands of divers, but it does not necessarily follow that even strict compliance with the tables will guarantee you immunity from a case of the bends. Susceptibility to decompression sickness varies with the individual. It even varies in the same individual on various days and under various conditions. To be 100 percent safe, the Decompression Tables would have to require such a long decompression time as to render them impractical. Therefore, whenever you use the U. S. Navy Standard Decompression Tables, it is always best to be conservative in figuring your decompression time. That is, it is always safe to decompress longer but never safe to decompress for less time than the tables call for.

Generally speaking, the individual is more susceptible to the bends, or decompression sickness, if he has overexerted himself on the dive, or suffers from a recent case of the bends, or from senility, obesity, lack of sleep, alcohol hangover, or anything else that might cause a generally poor physical or mental condition. However, most modern cases of decompression sickness have been caused by repetitive diving, that is, more than one dive in a twelve-hour period. Bearing in mind that it requires about twelve hours to desaturate a liquid of gas, when a diver makes more than one dive during any twelve-hour period the effect on the amount of gas in solution within the blood stream is cumulative, and the diver must follow an entirely different set of decompression tables called the Repetitive Dive Decompression Tables. These tables figure his "surface interval time" in relation to his total "down time" on both dives and spell out the safe decompression procedure for the second dive.

Because of the gravity of decompression sickness, you must plan all dives in which decompression becomes a factor with the utmost care. Be certain that you have more than enough air to support any decompression stops before you dive. The one cure for decompression sickness is to expose the victim as soon as possible to pressures at least as great as those of the deepest depth to which he was exposed during the dive.

Chapter 4

LEARNING TO SNORKEL DIVE

WHERE, WHEN, AND WITH WHOM

One of the cardinal rules of skin diving, whether it be with snorkel or scuba equipment, is *Never dive alone*. It is best to choose a diving buddy right at the outset, so you can begin your lessons and dive together as much as possible. Every person has his own peculiarities, and when you stick with the same diving buddy, you both soon get to know each other's abilities and limitations and can spot trouble the instant it approaches. Having a

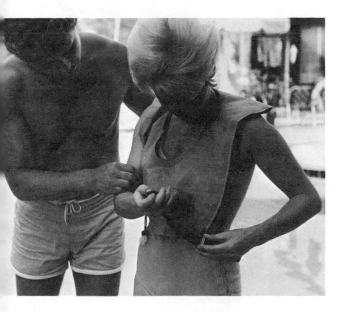

Learn to dive with a buddy.

good diving buddy, however, is no substitute for having a good instructor when you are learning. Your instructor should be a qualified teacher as well as a good diver. He should be certified by the National Association of Underwater Instructors (NAUWI) or the YMCA.

A baby must learn to crawl before he can walk or run, and the same slow beginning applies to diving. After requiring you to pass a test in basic swimming skills, your instructor will almost invariably teach you diving physiology first, and then will start you out in the shallow end of a swimming pool, or the shallow water of a protected beach. He will then, most likely, lead you through the following steps:

STEP 1: Equipment Familiarization

As described earlier, the basic equipment of a snorkel diver consists of a mask, snorkel, and fins, and, in open water, an inflating life vest or belt. When you are preparing to dive, the first thing you must do is attach the snorkel to the mask. Most snorkel tubes are equipped with a small rubber tab for this purpose. The tab loops around the strap of your face mask and thus holds it in place. Whether you affix the snorkel to the left side of your face mask or to the right side is immaterial; so long as the mouthpiece fits comfortably in your mouth, it is only a matter of personal preference.

Make sure snorkel fits mouth comfortably.

is done by simply spitting on the inside of the face plate, rubbing the saliva around the glass. In some mysterious way, the chemicals in your saliva prevent moisture from condensing on your faceplate and obscuring vision. (There are commercially produced defogging solutions, but nothing is so handy as spit, and you can't beat the price either.)

STEP 3: Testing for Leaks

After rinsing the mask, place it over your eyes and nose and inhale sharply. The mask should stay in place without the strap, because of the slight vacuum created by your inhalation. With the mask in place, put the strap over your head, adjust for comfort, and remove wrinkles or buckles. Insert the snorkel pipe between the mask strap and your temple. Then adjust the snorkel so that the mouthpiece fits comfortably. Place the two rubber bits between your teeth and the flanges between your teeth and lips.

STEP 2: Defogging the Mask

In the water, the warm moist air from your exhalation will condense on the inside of the faceplate of your mask unless you properly defog it before putting it on. This

Defog mask by rubbing saliva around faceplate.

Donning mask and snorkel ensemble.

Practice breathing through the snorkel for a while so that you become accustomed to it before getting in the water. Some people might think it difficult to breathe entirely through their mouths, but this feeling quickly passes when the mask is in place and they have no choice in the matter.

STEP 4: Donning the Fins

With the mask and snorkel in place, the prospective diver wets both feet and both fins; this permits the fins to slip easily over the foot without binding or catching. Insert your foot into the fin as far as it will go and then pull the heel of the fin up with your thumb. The fins should fit comfortably without binding or hurting in any way.

STEP 5: Entering the Water

When you have all your equipment on, the instructor teaches you how to enter the water. First, you will notice that walking with your fins on is very awkward. You must lift your feet high off the ground to prevent the blade of the fin from buckling and possibly tripping you. When you begin walking into the water, you will notice that the blade of the fin constantly buckles beneath your foot from the resistance of the water. Most instructors teach their students to enter the water backward, to lower the surface area of the fins offering resistance to the water.

STEP 6: Snorkel Breathing

Your instructor will ask you to lower your head into the water when the water is a few inches above your waist to accustom you to breathing through the snorkel while your face is submerged. This in itself is a new experience. Bend at the waist and submerge your face to the level of your ears. Then practice breathing. You will notice that, even though you are only partially submerged, the pressure of the water presses the mask against your face, creating

Donning fins.

Purging the snorkel of water.

a tight seal. You will also notice that no water leaks in around the snorkel in your mouth. While you are practicing breathing, develop the habit of inhaling very slowly and exhaling sharply. This will clear the snorkel tube of any water that might leak into it from the open end above your head. Now, try it floating on the surface of the water while pressing lightly against the bottom or hanging onto your instructor's hand to keep yourself afloat.

STEP 7: Clearing the Snorkel

Once you have mastered this, try ducking your head beneath the water, allowing your snorkel to fill. Then bring your head back to the surface and clear your snorkel. You will notice that, if you do not exhale with enough force, water will remain in the snorkel and you will choke on it when you inhale. This unpleasant experience quickly teaches you the proper technique for clearing the snorkel, and you will soon be snorkel breathing like a pro.

STEP 8: Clearing the Mask

If water leaks into your face mask, do not become alarmed. When snorkel diving, you are chained to the surface and must return

Clearing the face mask on the surface.

to it each time you want to take a new breath of air. Therefore it is a simple matter to lift the bottom edge of your face mask while on the surface and drain it of any water that may have accumulated there. Then try to replace the mask so that it has a better seal. Once you have committed yourself to the underwater world for longer periods with scuba gear, clearing your face mask of water becomes a different problem, but we shall deal with that when the time comes.

STEP 9: Snorkel Cruising

Once you accustom yourself to breathing through your snorkel, hang onto the edge of the pool or onto your instructor's hand or swimsuit and stretch out so that your body lies flat on the surface. Keep your face submerged in the water, practice kicking with your flippers, use the flutter kick just the way it is used in swimming the crawl stroke. Keep your knees as straight as possible, point your toes, and kick from the hips. Because of the greater surface area of the flippers, much more energy is required

Proper kick for snorkel cruising.

to move the flippers through the water than to move your naked feet. You will notice that your legs tire much more quickly as a result. This is natural. With a little practice, you will develop your leg muscles so that they can sustain kicking with the flippers for long periods of time without tiring.

When practicing flipper kicking, remember that the flippers can do no good unless they are completely submerged in the water. Therefore, be sure to kick so that only your heels, not the entire flipper, break the surface of the water. If the flipper leaves the water, you lose a good percentage of the power and efficiency of your kick. By raising your head slightly you lower your feet so that the flipper will remain submerged with each kick. You will also learn that it is not necessary to kick as rapidly with flippers as you would without them. A strong steady kick at a pace of no more than twenty per minute will drive you through the water at a good cruising rate without exhausting you. As you improve your technique you will notice that the flippers are so efficient that it becomes superfluous to use your arms. Any movement of your arms through the water while snorkel cruising simply creates added drag that slows you down. It is best to keep your arms glued next to your sides so as to streamline your body as much as possible. Later you will see that it is very convenient to have both hands free to spear fish, take pictures, or do some other kind of practical underwater work.

STEP 10:

Once you have developed the technique of snorkel cruising on the surface, it is time to learn to dive from the surface. There are three basic kinds of surface dives: the cannonball tuck, the pike tuck, and the feet-first dive. In any case, it is best to plan each dive. Lie flat and perfectly still on the surface of the water. Build up your supply of residual oxygen by breathing deeply several times, and think about what you want to do. Pick a target on the bottom so that you have some specific thing to look at on your way down; otherwise it is very easy to become disoriented once you get underwater. After you have planned your dive and hyperventilated a few times, exhale as much as you possibly can. Then inhale as much as you possibly can and hold it. Then go into your dive.

CANNONBALL TUCK

The easiest and most used dive is the cannonball tuck. As you take your last breath, give a powerful backward stroke with both hands while you tuck both knees up under your chest and roll your head and shoulders forward under the water. When your hips are directly over your head, straighten your legs out so that they stick straight up above the surface. The weight of your legs will drive you straight downward. Then reverse the stroke of your arms by bringing them from

Cannonball tuck dive—II.

Cannonball tuck dive—I.

in front of you sharply down to your sides. This helps to propel you to the bottom. Once your arms are by your sides keep them there until you reach the bottom by kicking. Any arm movement will create drag and possibly throw you off course.

As explained in the chapter on diving physiology, the deeper you go the longer you can stay without apparent discomfort or lack of air. Regardless of depth, because of the danger of shallow-water blackout during ascent, never willfully stay on the bottom more than a few seconds after you experience the first compulsive urge to breathe. By the time the second compulsive urge to breathe rolls around, you should already have pushed off the bottom on your ascent toward the surface. This is best done by crouching on the bottom and then pushing hard toward the surface with your feet while extending your arms above your head. When the glide is almost exhausted, bring your hands sharply down to your sides in a powerful breast stroke. For

The powerful porpoise kick is often used underwater.

over maneuver. After hyperventilating while floating on the surface in a spread-eagle position, bring your hands fully down to the sides. Then, pushing backward, bend at the waist, keeping your legs more or less straight. When your hips are directly over your head lift your legs up into the air just as in the cannonball tuck and begin to descend. The rest of the dive and recovery should be executed as in the cannonball dive.

the average depths of most beginning divers, this should bring you back to the surface without any further expenditure of energy. The moment you break the surface, exhale sharply through your snorkel tube. This will clear (purge) the water from the tube so that you can inhale immediately afterward.

PIKE TUCK

The pike tuck is executed much like the cannonball tuck, except for the initial roll-

Pike tuck dive—I.

Pike tuck dive—II.

FEET-FIRST DIVE

The feet-first dive is used almost exclusively in spearfishing, when the splashing from the tuck or cannonball dives might frighten a prize fish out of spear range. Begin this dive

Feet-first dive—I.

from a vertical position in the water. With a powerful kick of your flippers, rise out of the water up to your chest. When the weight of the exposed portion of your body overbalances the thrust of the kick, reverse the direction of your movement, and you will begin to sink. At this instant, bring your arms sharply upward in a reverse kind of breast stroke, driving yourself farther beneath the surface. Once beneath the surface, roll over, so that you can continue the descent head first throughout the remainder of the dive. The ascent is made exactly as in the tuck and cannonball techniques.

When jumping in, hold equipment in place during entry.

Feet-first dive—II.

STEP 11: Equalizing

During your initial dive, you will experience such ear pain from the rapidly increasing water pressure that you will not be able to dive much deeper than ten or fifteen feet. Certainly you could will yourself to proceed in spite of the pain, but this is inadvisable, for you would run the risk of rupturing an eardrum if you did. Once you learn how to equalize or clear your ears, however, the only limit to the depth you can dive will be your ability to hold your breath.

The basic technique for clearing the ears is described in the chapter on diving physiology. It involves pinching off your nostrils and snorting air through the Eustachian tubes that lead from your nasal passages into your inner ear. This equalizes the air pressure in your inner ear with the sur-

Diving safety depends primarily on your own common sense. Photo Ron Church

Advanced snorkelers often go spearfishing for added thrills. Photo Victor De Sanctis

rounding water pressure. Many modern face masks are molded with cavities that fit on either side of the nose to facilitate pinching off your nostrils for the ear-clearing procedure. If your face mask does not have this built-in facility you must press the bottom of the mask up against your nose before snorting in order to prevent the air from escaping into the mask. When you succeed in clearing your ears, you will actually hear the air rush through your Eustachian tubes and feel instant relief.

You will be able to proceed until the ear pain begins to bother you again, at which point you must repeat the ear-clearing procedure. If one ear clears and the other does not, do not try to force it. Ascend a few feet to relieve the pressure and then try again.

If you are a beginner or have not dived in a long time, it is best to open your Eustachian tubes by clearing or "popping"

your ears at a couple of practice sessions before you reach the water. This can be done by simply pinching off your nostrils and snorting air into your inner ear as you normally would in the water. However, this must be done with great caution, for it is possible to burst your eardrum if done too forcefully. If you have difficulty in clearing your ears, try swallowing or working your jaws up and down at the same time you snort. Once having gotten the air inside your inner ear, you need not worry about getting rid of it. The pressure in your inner ear will equalize automatically during ascent, for the air exits from your Eustachian tubes much more easily than it enters.

One other word of caution—head colds cause the Eustachian tubes to swell and fill with mucus and often make it virtually impossible to clear your ears. For this reason, it is best not to dive at all so long as you suffer from a cold.

Captain Arthur Watkins and author with results of fifteen minutes of snorkeling off the Caicos Islands. Photo Esther Watkins

Dreamlike and weightless: like a bird in the sky! Photo Owen Lee

Chapter 5

LEARNING TO SCUBA DIVE

WHERE, WHEN, AND WITH WHOM

After requiring you to pass a test in diving physiology and basic snorkel diving, your instructor will probably return you to the same shallow end of the swimming pool or beach where you began and introduce you to the techniques of scuba diving. He will then, most likely, lead you through the following steps:

STEP 1: Equipment Familiarization

In addition to the basic equipment of the snorkel diver—that is, mask, snorkel, and fins—the scuba diver must have a tank of compressed air, a breathing regulator, and an air pressure gauge. If the temperature of the water warrants it, he must also have a wet-type rubber exposure suit and a quick-release belt of lead weights to counteract the buoyancy of the suit.

In snorkel diving you have already learned how to check and adjust your mask, snorkel, and fins. Once you have them properly adjusted, they should remain that way until you change them. Since your life will depend upon your scuba equipment while you are submerged, you must also be certain that it fits and functions properly. Therefore, before you enter the water, spread your equipment out before you and inspect it as follows:

1. Check the air pressure in your tanks with your pressure gauge, even though you may have just filled them. Make sure they are at least 70 percent full before you enter the water.

2. Check the position of the air reserve lever, if any. Make sure it is in the closed or "up" position.

3. Check the back-pack and harness assembly of your air tank. Make sure the tank is securely fastened and that the harness

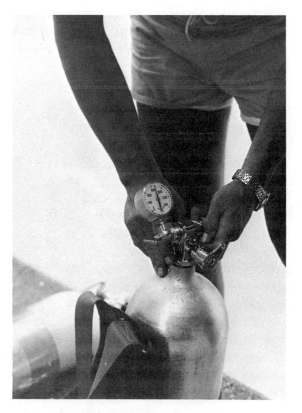

Check your air pressure.

Check the regulator and valve for leaks.

4. Check the breathing regulator for leaks by inhaling strongly through the mouthpiece while the protective cap still seals the high-pressure stage. If you receive air, check the hose for leaks, especially around the connecting joints. If you cannot find any in the hose, remove the regulator housing and check the rubber diaphragm for leaks. *Do not dive with a leaking regulator.*

5. Attach the regulator to the air tank and check the seating by opening the tank valve and listening for leaks. If you are not sure, submerge the valve and regulator in water and look for bubbles.

6. Check the air flow by inserting the mouthpiece and breathing from it. Air flow should start easily and stop completely after each exhalation.

straps do not have dangerous worn spots. Adjust the harness straps for a comfortable fit and see that all couplings are made with quick-release hitches.

Check the regulator air flow.

Check your suit for tears.

7. Check your rubber suit for tears or weak spots. Repair if necessary while the suit is still dry.

8. Check your weight belt for neutral buoyancy by adding or subtracting weights while you are floating in the water. (When properly weighted for neutral buoyancy, you should gently sink after exhaling and gently float after inhaling.)

Don your gear the easy way.

Check your weights for neutral buoyancy.

STEP 2: Donning Equipment

If everything checks out, the equipment should be donned in the following sequence: suit (if any), flotation vest, tank and regulator assembly, weight belt (if any), fins and mask.

Sprinkle the inside of your suit liberally with talcum or its equivalent to prevent the rubber from binding or catching on your skin when you slip it on. When you are all suited up, the easiest way to get into your scuba harness is to have your buddy help you into it as he might help you into a top-

coat. If your buddy is lazy, hateful, or otherwise not predisposed to helping, you can get into your scuba harness by yourself. The step-by-step procedure of this heroic "don-it-yourself" maneuver is illustrated in the photo series on pages 70–71.

Once you have donned the heavy air tank, you are bound to be top heavy and easily thrown off balance, especially on the pitching deck of a boat. The clumsy flippers only aggravate the problem of equilibrium, so sit on something solid while you don your flippers and mask and remain seated, if possible, until you are ready to enter the water.

To don your flippers, wet your feet so they will not bind on the rubber and then jam your foot into the shoe of the flipper as you stand on its blade with the other foot or otherwise prevent it from slipping away. Then reach down and draw the heel of the flipper over the heel of your foot with your fingers. If you are seated on a deck or a beach you can put your flippers on as you might put on a pair of shoes.

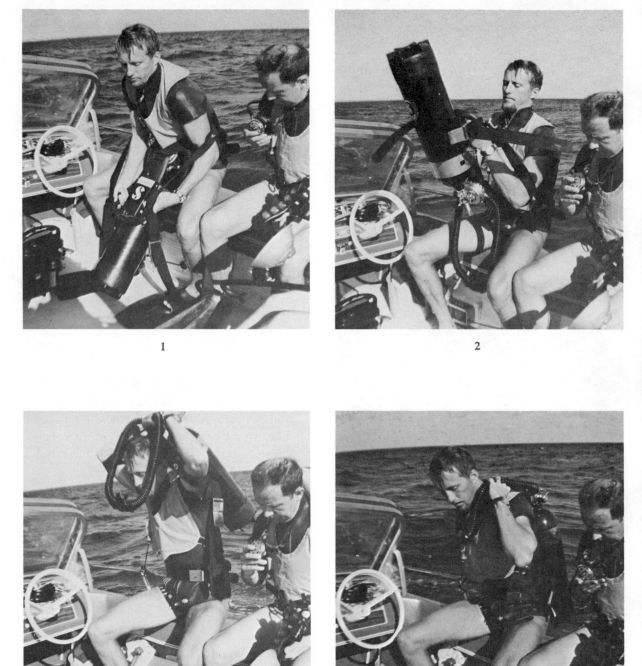

1

2

3

4

Here's how to don it yourself. Courtesy Underwater Explorer's Club, Grand Bahama

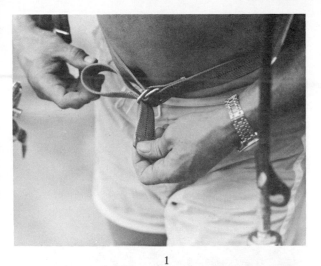

1

2

Quick-release buckle facilitates quick exit from gear in case of emergency.

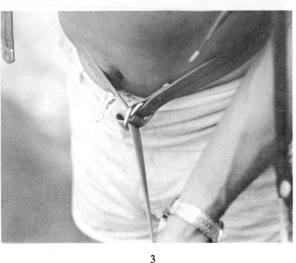

3

STEP 3: Entering and Leaving the Water

The proverbial fish-out-of-water is only slightly more pathetic than the diver fully suited up and ready to dive. He is awkward, hot, and uncomfortable. But once he enters the water, he can be as free and as graceful as a fish. Therefore, once you are suited up and ready you should head for the water as soon as possible, with the least possible last-minute dilly-dallying around.

As in snorkel diving, climbing up or down a ladder or wading backward on a beach is the easiest and most practical way to enter or leave the water. This is, no doubt, how your instructor will have you enter and leave the water for your first scuba lesson. However, entering and leaving the water are often the most taxing parts of a dive. Most divers like to get it over with as soon as possible, so they usually enter by either jumping in or rolling in—they *never dive head first*.

I should mention here that the sudden pressure change resulting from jumping in is hard on the sinuses, but occasions arise when you have little choice in your method

Wade in and out of the water backward when wearing fins.

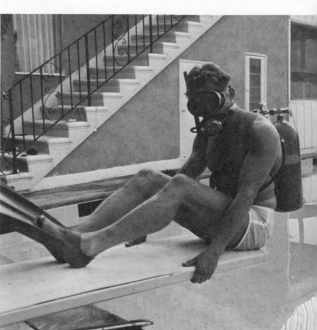

Feet-first-jump with scuba gear.

Back roll-in entry. Practice first at the pool.

of entry, and so it is best that you learn to execute the jump entries.

The most commonly used method of entry is the *feet first jump*. To execute this, stand erect on gunwale or deck and after making sure that you have a clear landing area and enough water beneath, steady your face mask with one hand and the lower end of the air tank with the other so that it cannot ride up and hit you in the back of the head. Then simply step out into space, entering the water vertically.

Standing on the gunwale of a pitching boat poised to jump feet first is not easy. In choppy water, divers usually use the *back roll-in entry*. Execute this by facing the middle of the boat and sitting, back to the water, as close to the edge of the gunwale as possible. Steady the mask and tank as described above and simply lean back over the water until the weight of the tank pulls you in. It is important that the tank be completely clear of the gunwale or deck and your feet completely clear of your buddy's chin before you begin your roll in.

The *side roll-in entry,* a variation of the *back roll-in,* is often used in very rough water. Instead of sitting on the gunwale or

edge of the deck, crawl up to it on all fours. Then fall sideways over the edge of the boat, steadying your mask and tank before you hit the water.

Leaving the water is not quite so simple as entering it. After the dive, you will usually be exhausted, and pulling yourself onto a boat or deck while wearing heavy diving equipment is a Herculean task. A deep, sturdy boarding ladder is the obvious solution. A boatswain's chair, Jacob's ladder, cargo net, or knotted rope hung over the side will also facilitate exit from the water. But even when these are available, it is always best to remove your heavy, cumbersome equipment before you attempt to leave the water. Hanging onto the ladder or a rope, first remove your weight belt and hand it to a helper on deck. Do the same with your flippers, for they have a nasty habit of buckling under your feet on the rungs of the ladder. Men can usually manage to climb aboard without removing their

Back roll-in entry from a boat. Photo Jack McKenney

air tanks, but if you are a woman or are exhausted, unbuckle your tank harness and have it lifted aboard before you exit, especially if the boat is rolling.

STEP 4: Scuba Breathing

Standing in waist-deep water, your instructor will ask you to put your face mask and mouthpiece in place and then accustom yourself to breathing through the scuba above water. Then he will ask you to submerge your face in the water and continue breathing through the scuba while you hang on to him or to your buddy. If you are like most people, you will feel that it is impossible to either inhale or exhale the moment your face hits the water. This is normal· after years of believing that it is impossible to breathe underwater. However, I assure you that it is all in your mind. Your scuba will permit you to breathe normally underwater just as soon as you begin to believe it will.

Once you overcome this hurdle, the sensation of being able to breathe underwater will be so thrilling that you will want to go spinning off in all directions. Resist this urge for a while and content yourself with ducking your head deeper underwater by walking your hands down your instructor's or buddy's leg until you reach his ankles. Then just hang on and breathe. When you are thoroughly convinced that your scuba really works, you can let go and begin to swim along the bottom, feeling it out very cautiously. If you pop to the surface in spite of yourself the moment you let go, your instructor will give you enough weight to keep you neutrally buoyant. Swim side by side with your buddy back and forth along the bottom until you are thoroughly accustomed to the sensation. Then return to the surface, and practice making surface dives to the bottom just as you learned to do in snorkel diving. As you gain proficiency, try diving deeper and deeper until at last the pain in your ears tells you that you had better clear your ears before proceeding any farther.

Caution. Always remember how Boyle's Law of Gases applies to you. Never hold your breath while changing depths if you

Get the feel of scuba breathing.

Equalizing ears.

are breathing compressed air, for you will run the risk of suffering squeeze (page 149) or, worse yet, air embolism. Always breathe normally when changing depth levels, especially during ascent.

STEP 5: Equalizing (Clearing) Your Ears

Clearing your ears is much easier when you are diving with scuba than with a snorkel, because you have a supply of precompressed air to do the job. Unlike snorkel diving, if at first you don't succeed, simply take another breath and try again. The compressed air supply also allows you to begin clearing earlier in your descent so that your Eustachian tubes will not be squeezed shut by the pressure before equalization can be completed. For this reason, it is advisable to begin clearing the moment you dive and to continue snorting, swallowing, or wiggling your jaws throughout your descent to the bottom.

Clearing the ears during repetitive dives is sometimes difficult because of an accumulation of mucus in the Eustachian tubes from previous dives. However, generally speaking, the more you dive, the more easily you can clear.

STEP 6: Clearing Your Mask

Regardless of how well your mask fits over your face, some water is bound to leak inside sooner or later. This causes discomfort and distorted vision. Furthermore, it would be senseless to return to the surface every time you needed to clear your mask of water as you might normally do while snorkel diving. Therefore, clearing the mask while underwater is a basic skill of the scuba diver.

To understand the principle of clearing your mask while underwater, try this experiment: plunge an ordinary drinking glass into a tub of water, and allow it to flood. Then hold the glass vertical in the water, open end down. Now bend the end of a drinking straw so that it is shaped like a fishhook and hook it around the open end of the glass so that one end emerges from the water far enough to permit blowing through it. Blow through the straw and you will see air accumulate at the top of the glass. It quickly drives the water inside the glass out the bottom until the glass is filled with air down to the level of the opening of the straw. In clearing your mask of water, you follow the same "diving bell principle." However, instead of using a straw, you simply roll your head backward so that your faceplate is parallel with the surface of the water. Then holding (not pressing) the mask in place you blow air into it by exhaling through your nose. The water will go out the bottom of the mask. You will find, with practice, that one exhalation is all you need to completely clear your mask of water. However, if one exhalation is not enough to do the job, take another breath and repeat the procedure until your mask is clear of water. The salt in seawater may cause a slight stinging sensation in your nose and eyes, but it can't hurt you and water cannot enter your nose unless you inhale through it.

As you gain proficiency, you will find it unnecessary to roll all the way back to make the faceplate absolutely parallel with the surface. By holding the top of your mask in place with your fingers, you can roll your head back or to either side so that the faceplate is just slightly off vertical and accomplish the same thing. The important thing is to maintain a tight seal at the upper edge of the mask to prevent the air's escaping except at the bottom. Many of the new and more expensive face masks are equipped not only with a nose-pinching device to help clear the ears but with a one-way exhaust valve that allows water to leave the mask but prevents it from entering. This purging valve obviates the need to roll over on your back or side to utilize the "diving bell principle." By simply exhaling through your nose into the mask, you keep the mask clear and dry. When you are learning, it is best to familiarize yourself with the mask-clearing process by diving to the bottom, removing the mask, and then replacing and clearing it while

Clearing mask with "top purge."

Clearing mask with "side purge."

underwater. When you have practiced this, you can carry the idea further while you are on the surface: throw your mask into the water several yards away from you, swim underwater, retrieve it, put it on, and clear it.

STEP 7: Clearing the Mouthpiece

It is a common practice for experienced divers to remove and replace their scuba mouthpiece while underwater. To remove or replace a camera strap around the neck, to fill a lifting bag with air from the air tank, or to give a buddy air (buddy breathing) are just a few reasons for doing so. However, the most common reason is the involuntary one of having your mouthpiece yanked from your mouth accidentally by catching your air hose on an object. Therefore, it is essential that you learn how to recover a lost mouthpiece and clear it of water while totally submerged.

The mouthpieces of all modern breathing regulators are equipped with nonreturn valves that prevent water from entering the feeder hose leading from the tank to the diver's mouth. Water can enter only the small confines of the mouthpiece itself and · this is easily cleared by inserting the mouthpiece and exhaling sharply. All modern single-hose, two-stage regulators are equipped with a purge button which, when pressed, mechanically opens the intake valve and allows a free flow of air to escape from the feeder hose. This automatically clears the regulator mouthpiece of water, so that the diver can then inhale almost pure air. I say "almost pure air" because a few drops of water are likely to remain in the mouthpiece after direct exposure to the water. Therefore, after clearing the mouthpiece of water, the diver's next inhalation should be executed slowly and cautiously as he faces the bottom, so that the few remaining droplets of water will fall away from the mouthpiece and be blown out

through the exhaust valve with the next exhalation. If a small amount of water is inadvertently drawn into your mouth, don't fight it. Swallow it. If you accidentally lose your mouthpiece underwater, it almost invariably flies over your head because of the buoyancy created by the free flow of air that is released. To find it, you should instinctively reach over your head. If by chance it is not there, reach behind you to your tank valve and follow the hose up to the mouthpiece with your hand. Then, by rolling your head back and keeping the mouthpiece pointed downward (toward your mouth), you can cause the free flow of air bubbling out through your mouthpiece to clear the mouthpiece of water automatically. You then need only to insert it into your mouth to begin breathing. This procedure works equally well with the single-hose or double-hose regulator and is especially good to remember when you have lost your mouthpiece just after exhaling.

STEP 8: Buddy Breathing

Buddy breathing consists in two or more divers breathing from one scuba. It is an emergency procedure that should never have to be used except in the unlikely case of total and abrupt equipment failure. In such cases, *free ascent,* much more dangerous, is the only alternative, and so it is wise to learn and practice buddy breathing just in case. If nothing else, it will develop skill in clearing your mouthpiece and teach you the value of diving with a buddy.

Once you get the hang of it, the most difficult part of buddy breathing is making known your need to do it. In time of real emergency, the best method of accomplishing this is the one that is sure to work quickly.

Circumstances would dictate what precisely that might be, but if I may venture a guess, it would most likely be swimming to your buddy and tugging at his mouthpiece

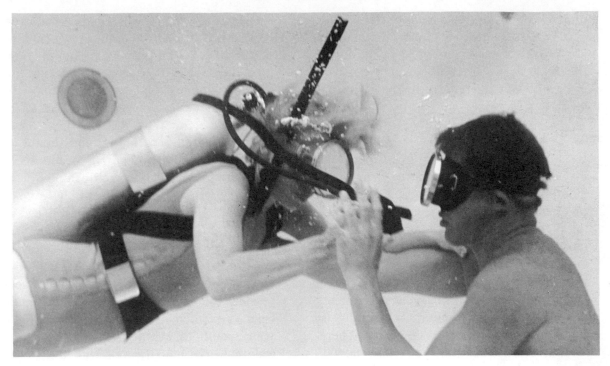

Buddy breathing.

while frantically wiping your finger across your throat in the "cut-throat" gesture and pointing to your mouth. However, in practice sessions it is best to follow protocol:

1. Attract your buddy's attention.

2. Tell him your air supply is out by wiping your finger across your throat.

3. Indicate you want to buddy breathe with him by pointing to his mouthpiece and then to your mouth.

4. Get into position by putting his left hand on your right shoulder and putting your left hand on his right shoulder.

5. Take your buddy's mouthpiece from his mouth with your free right hand and insert it into yours as you start kicking for the surface together.

6. Clear the mouthpiece, take three or four deep breaths, and hand the mouthpiece back to your buddy; he then does the same thing while you slowly exhale in preparation for repeating the cycle.

7. Repeat the last two steps until you reach the surface. Since you are ascending,

remember to avoid holding your breath. When not actually inhaling, you should be slowly but continuously exhaling.

In practice sessions, buddy breathe while swimming back and forth along the bottom of the pool. When this becomes too easy to be challenging, invite others to join you in a "Buddy Breathing Buster." As they sit in a circle on the bottom of the pool, see how many divers you can get breathing from the same scuba before someone has to break for the surface.

Caution: Exhale while ascending!

STEP 9: Doffing and Donning

Doffing and donning is a drill designed to develop skill and confidence in yourself and your equipment. In practice, most instructors require students to place all their scuba equipment, including mask, snorkel, and fins, under a weight belt in the deep end of a pool. Then the students are required to swim underwater to their equipment from the shallow end of the pool (or beach

HOW TO DITCH EQUIPMENT AND MAKE FREE ASCENT

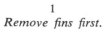

1

Remove fins first.

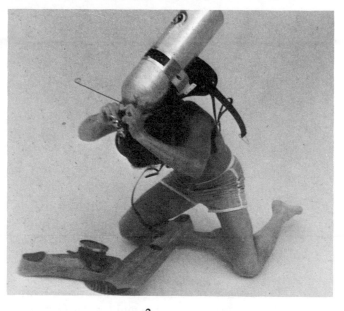

2

Remove back-pack. Keep breathing.

3

Take your last breath.

4

REMEMBER TO EXHALE COMPLETELY DURING ASCENT.

run), don their equipment, swim several lengths of the pool with the equipment on, and then return to the deep end, doff their equipment, and return to the shallow end, *all without breaking the surface.*

As you approach your equipment, the first thing you must do is open the air valve of your tank, insert the mouthpiece, clear it, and begin breathing. Then, draping your weight belt over your thighs so that you won't have to fight to stay down, place your face mask properly, and clear it of water so that you can see. Don your air tank with the overhead lift as illustrated on page 70 and buckle your harness. Buckle your weight belt and put on your fins before you begin to swim.

At the end of the drill, you simply reverse the procedure. First remove your fins; then unbuckle your weight belt. Unbuckle your harness and doff your tank by pitching forward and swinging the tank over your head, but do not let go of the mouthpiece until you doff your face mask, hyperventilate, take a last deep breath of air, and shut the tank valve. Then take off for the shallow end, being careful to allow some of the air to escape as you gradually ascend toward the surface.

STEP 10: Blind Diving

Many instructors put their students through a blind-diving drill, to acquaint them with the inevitable underwater sensation of being weightless without being able to see. I say "inevitable" because the slightest disturbance underwater can raise a cloud of silt that will suddenly turn your underwater environment black as night. In addition you may be asked to perform in water so murky that your sense of sight becomes useless. Therefore, it is advisable that you learn to "see" underwater through your sense of touch.

This drill is practiced by first placing a piece of cardboard over the inside of your faceplate before donning the mask. Then your instructor will ask you to submerge, swim several lengths of the pool, find some object that is anchored on the bottom, and perform some minor task with it before returning to the surface.

Needless to say, blind diving is a weird sensation. In your weightless state it is difficult to tell which direction is "up" unless you feel the direction of your bubbles or note which way you tend to float when inhaling deeply. When you are swimming blind underwater, it is best not to break contact with the bottom. By dragging one hand along the bottom and swimming along the edge of the pool, you can maintain direction. However, always protect your head by extending your other hand out in front of you, and breathe normally throughout the drill to avoid air embolism.

If you pass this test, the chances are that you are ready for an open-water dive. However, there is one experience you will encounter at the end of every dive that we have not touched upon yet. Therefore, you should experience it now! That is . . .

STEP 11: Exhausting Your Air Supply

At least twice during your early training, you should remain submerged with scuba until you run out of air: once with an air tank equipped with a constant-reserve J valve and once with an air tank equipped with a straight K (no reserve) valve. This is an experience that you are bound to encounter if you continue diving, and it will demonstrate the characteristics of each kind of air-flow valve that you are most likely to use.

In both cases, you will note that the air does not exhaust itself abruptly but that breathing becomes gradually more difficult until you either ascend toward the surface or, if your tank has a J valve, you pull your reserve lever. If you ascend, the decreasing ambient air pressure will allow the residual air in your tank to expand and provide you with a breath or two more of air, according to Boyle's Law of Gases. This applies to tanks equipped with either J or K valves. By opening the reserve on your J-valve tank, you release 300 p.s.i.a. of air that is held in check by a spring-loaded valve mechanism. The duration of this 300 p.s.i.a. reserve will vary in direct proportion to your depth, according to Boyle's Law. In any case, the J-valve reserve permits you to go deeper before you begin your ascent, as one might be forced to do in wreck or cave diving, for example. Once the air has been exhausted from the straight K-valve tank, you have little choice but to go straight up.

Having experienced exhausted air supply two or three times, you are ready for your first open-water dive.

Make your first open-water dive in clear, warm water if possible. Photo Underwater Explorer's Club, Freeport, Grand Bahama

Keep a sharp eye out for danger. Photo Jack McKenney

Chapter 6

DIVING HAZARDS

It's a fact that God gave the sea to fishes. You cannot really get indignant with a hungry shark that thinks you are a fish and bites you. Nor can you get angry with a sea urchin for your having stepped on him after intruding into his home, as it were. Although there are a few sea creatures that can be aggressively dangerous, most potentially dangerous sea creatures are totally passive in nature. In either case, it behooves you as a visitor to respect their right of eminent domain in the underwater world and actively avoid them. They can be classified into two categories: predatory sea creatures and venomous sea creatures.

PREDATORY SEA CREATURES

In one way or another, all creatures that live in the sea are predatory. Whether actively or passively, all subsist on other forms of life that live in the sea, and the secret of underwater longevity is simply to eat without being eaten. However, this does not mean that all sea creatures are aggressively hostile or even dangerous. They hunt only when they are hungry. Furthermore, they are selective in their prey. If given a choice, all sea creatures, even sharks, would prefer sea food to terrestrial food, such as man. The smell of human blood does not even start their gastric juices flowing, whereas the mere whiff of fish blood might trigger a hysterical feeding frenzy. Of this you can be sure: if any sea creature attacks a human being in the water, it is a case of mistaken identity, usually due to obscured vision or confusion, revenge for a provocative act of aggression or molestation, or an act of desperation due to the fact that it has become too old or ill to compete for its food on a normal basis.

Although chemically different from our own, the sea is anything but a hostile environment. If approached with a minimum of respect, it can be an amiable place of enchantment, beauty, and endless opportunity. Its generosity to man knows no limit, yet it takes nothing from man but abuse. Thus you may enter the watery realm with no more apprehension than you might experience when visiting a strange town or taking your first airplane ride. With the possible exception of the Orca, all sea creatures are basically unaggressive.

The Orca or Killer Whale

It should immediately be explained that the Orca or killer whale—the only exception to this rule—is not a fish but an air-breathing mammal, a member of the otherwise friendly porpoise family. Once a terrestrial animal like man, the Orca's ancestor moved into the sea millions of years ago and apparently liked it so well that it never came back. Like man, it is chained to the atmosphere it breathes. As

Orca or killer whale. Courtesy of the American Museum of Natural History

a result, it lives a nomadic life at the sea's surface. Unlike most men, however, it has a propensity for cold water. It favors the arctic latitudes, although it ventures as far south as Cape Hatteras on the East Coast and Southern California on the West Coast.

It is fortunate that Orcas are relatively rare in U.S. waters, for it is commonly believed that their aggressiveness is not limited to sea creatures but to anything that walks, crawls, or swims. Because of its voracious appetite and its predilection for wanton killing even when not feeding, it has won the title of "Killer of the Seas." This and its superior intelligence, cunning, and size make it the most fearsome animal on land or sea.

In 1956 an Orca was taken into captivity for the first time, in Seattle, Washington. In order to keep their prized tourist attraction alive and well publicized, divers were obliged to enter the Orca's crib to feed it and photograph it. One of them, cinematographer La-

mar Boren, reported the Orca to be surprisingly docile; perhaps its reputation as a killer is in for some serious revision. Meanwhile, better be safe than sorry. Avoid the Orca at all costs. Leave the water as soon as one is sighted.

Female Orcas range in length from ten to twenty feet, while the males grow as large as thirty feet long and weigh several tons. The Orca can easily be identified at a distance by the huge black dorsal fin, which protrudes high above the water as it swims. At closer range its husky streamlined body appears black on top, with a white belly and a white patch above the eye.

Sharks

Although it is not entirely justified, the shark's reputation as a killer rivals that of the Orca. Whenever a real shark attack occurs, it makes such dramatic newscopy that prac-

Great white shark. Courtesy of the American Museum of Natural History

tically everybody hears about it and most people believe, erroneously, that sharks attack all human beings on sight. The fact is that the number of shark attacks compared with the number of shark encounters is minute.

If bold and persistent enough, most saltwater divers eventually encounter a shark, and the experience invariably marks a milestone in their diving career. Many a shark has turned a hairy-chested diver into a chicken of the sea. A shark encounter has brought to some a sudden ability almost to run (not walk) on water. Shark encounters are a good test of a diver's enthusiasm. If he ever dives again after his first shark encounter, he is likely to continue diving forever.

Many qualified people, both privately and in organized groups, have studied sharks to define their behavioral patterns, and a few have met with a certain measure of success. It has been found that all sharks are able to sense the convulsions of a dying fish from distances of over half a mile. This is accomplished by a set of tiny disks and hairlike receptors, called *lateral lines,* running from the nostrils down the sides of sharks and other pelagic fishes. A diver who spears a fish in shark-infested waters *can expect* the arrival of sharks in five to twenty minutes unless

his spear hits the fish in the brain or backbone and effects an "instant kill." The shark homes in on the vibrations until he picks up the scent of fish blood. The scent of fish blood starts the shark's gastric juices flowing and induces a radical change in behavior. (*Note:* The shark is basically a fish eater, not a human eater. Since human or animal blood is likely to be a new experience not associated with feeding, it probably will not affect the shark in the same way as fish blood.) Instead of casually circling around in curious perusal, as he usually does, the shark will swim about with abrupt and erratic movements. He is likely to thrash his head from side to side to see where the blood is coming from. He is likely to dart up to investigate anything curious. If he sees a fish, he is likely to attack it. If he sees you *with* the fish or you *instead* of the fish, he might attack you!

Sharks in pairs or in groups are extremely dangerous in this "feeding mood." They appear to stimulate each other into bolder acts— probably because they are competing for the same food. If one attacks, the others are almost sure to follow.

But after all their research, scientists can only affirm that a shark's behavior is entirely unpredictable. Shark behavior is rarely the same, even among the same species. All the sharks I have encountered have spent considerable time circling me curiously with only occasional sorties in close for an intimate look at their prospective meal. The one that did attack (after stupid provocation) even stopped and maneuvered into position before he struck. Yet most shark-attack victims report that they never saw the shark before the attack. Almost invariably, however, fish had been caught or speared in the area.

The exception to this is the rogue shark or, as treasure-diver Teddy Tucker of Bermuda calls it, the *great gentleman*. He is an outcast, usually a huge specimen too senile or ill to compete for his food with other sharks and fishes. He is reduced to prowling the more offbeat places where food, though less choice, perhaps, is more easily come by: sewage outlets, ship and garbage dumps, and sheltered beaches. He may even be reduced to eating something other than the fish he prefers . . . like you!

The best way to avoid attack, of course, is to avoid sharks. Stay away from places that sharks are known to frequent—especially waste disposal areas. Be sure to boat or bag all speared fish immediately, and make sure that the bag has no holes through which fish blood might leak into the water. If you insist on using a fish stringer, tie it to the end of a long, long line. Never tie it close to your body. Fish only during flood tides so that fish blood is washed shoreward. Don't gut or clean fish until all divers are out of the area. Don't dangle your feet in the water from a boat. If you are snorkel diving, return to the surface after each dive, spiraling around in circles as you go to give yourself a 360-degree sweep of the water. If a shark comes in anyway, don't freeze in fear or splash on the surface. Stay near the bottom and look alive and aggressive as you swim steadily for your boat. If the shark gets too curious, make an aggressive lunge at him. Hit him in the snoot with something solid (other than your fist) if

possible. In any case, always swim with a buddy. The shark can only eat one person at a time. Maybe he will go for your buddy first and give you time to climb on the boat.

Barracuda

The barracuda, also, enjoys a highly overrated reputation for viciousness, but it is one of my favorite reef fishes. As fish go, it somehow comes across to me as being much more *macho,* as the Spanish say, than most. It frequents tropical waters and has a beautiful streamlined, cigar-shaped body that ranges in size from two to seven feet in length, with a doglike jaw full of razor-sharp teeth. When necessary, it can move through the water with the speed of lightning. However, it usually loafs in the shade beneath boats or piers or lurks practically motionless in the water near coral formations.

Much of the barracuda's ferocious reputation probably stems from its insatiable curiosity. Many divers have been startled out of their wits by the discovery of an unsuspected barracuda peering over their shoulder trying to see what they are up to. When the diver chases them off, they become highly indignant, gnashing their teeth and sometimes shuddering in rage like a cantankerous old man. But this is more a bullish show of frustration than a threat. When the diver returns to his business, the barracuda usually settles down and resumes following him curiously but from a greater distance. Finally it gets bored and continues about its fishy business.

Almost invariably, barracuda attacks on human beings have occurred in murky water, where the hands or feet of a swimmer or diver in action, being only partially visible, might have given the impression of being a small fish moving quickly through the water. Barracudas are easily excited by quick movements or shiny fishy-looking objects and may strike at them impulsively. Therefore, avoid swimming in murky waters, don't wear shiny ob-

Barracuda.

jects, and swim with slow, steady movements; you then are never likely to feel the barracuda's teeth.

Eels

There are a number of eel species and they range in size from the small spotted moray eel that measures about two feet in length to the South Pacific brown moray that measures up to ten feet. In between there are the slimy green moray that is around six feet long, the stubby black electric eel, around four feet long, and the powerful conger eel and wolf eel that measure up to eight feet in length. They all share a predilection for seclusion, preferring the dark holes and crevasses of the reefs, coral heads, and rock jetties to the open water. They will bother no one unless they are provoked or intruded upon. Most eel bites have resulted from divers reaching into a dark hole for a lobster who happened to share his habitat with an eel. Once the eel bites, however, it clings tenaciously, and severing the back of its head is often the only way to loosen its grip. When under threat of death, it will strike indiscriminately at anything within reach and give you a dramatic demonstration of the meaning of the word writhing.

Look before you poke your head or arm into any dark holes in reefs, wrecks, or jetties. If you spear an eel, hold your spear firmly and keep it at a distance until he is subdued. The eel's teeth are covered with an in-

Eel. Courtesy of the American Museum of Natural History

fectious slime. If you are bitten, your wound is likely to become infected unless you wash, soak, and disinfect it thoroughly as soon as possible.

VENOMOUS CREATURES OF THE SEA

Though less dramatic and less consequential than contacts with predatory sea creatures, contacts with venomous animals of the sea are likely to be much more frequent. The Office of Naval Research, in collaboration with Dr. Paul Rom Saunders of the Biology Department of the University of Southern California, compiled a list of the venomous sea creatures so that naval personnel might avoid them. With their permission I quote from their list for your information.

Certain creatures of the sea can inflict in man venomous wounds resulting in serious injury or even death in some cases. In contrast to our extensive knowledge of the venoms of terrestrial animals, relatively little is known about the nature and actions of marine animal venoms. Consequently, the treatment of injuries resulting from such wounds is usually empirical and often ineffective.

Stonefish

The stonefish is one of those animals. It is one of many marine bony fishes that possess venomous spines. When erected the spines penetrate the skin easily. Wounds cause agonizing pain and swelling, and in severe cases produce cardiovascular collapse and death.

The stonefish is found in shallow water in many parts of the tropical Pacific and Indian Oceans. Usually less than a foot long, it is commonly found partially buried in the sand, and is extremely difficult to see. Injuries often occur when a person accidentally steps upon the fish.

This fish must be considered one of the most dangerous of the marine animals. Each of the thirteen individual spines of the dorsal fin is covered by a thick sheath of tissue. This sheath is pressed down upon the underlying venom sacs upon contact. The resulting pressure causes the fluid venom to be forced into the puncture wound produced.

Removal of the outer sheath reveals on either side of the spine the two venom sacs, each containing a small drop or less of venom. A duct leads to the tip of the spine.

Lion-fish

Another dangerous bony fish found in the tropical Indo-Pacific is known variously as the lion-fish, turkey fish, zebra fish or by other names. This member of the scorpion-fish family reaches a length of about one foot, and is most commonly seen in shallow water swimming about slowly or resting on coral formations or in caves.

The lion-fish is readily visible and injuries often result from the careless handling of captured specimens. Wounds are usually inflicted by the long banded dorsal spines. The covering thin tissue sheath tears when the spine penetrates the flesh, and venom from the underlying spaces enters the wound.

Symptoms produced are similar to those caused by stonefish stings. Serious systemic effects are less common but a marked fall in blood pressure to dangerous levels has occurred.

Like the stonefish, this animal is not known to use its spines as offensive weapons in the capture of prey, but secures its food in the usual manner. The biological function of the venom apparatus in this fish, and in the stonefish, is unknown, although it may play a role as a defensive weapon.

Scorpion Fish

The California scorpion fish also possesses venomous spines on its dorsal fin which can be erected when the fish is disturbed. Wounds, usually due to careless handling by fishermen, cause severe pain and swelling, although serious systemic effects are rare.

Rays

Certain cartilaginous fishes are also venomous, and of this group the most numerous are various rays.

Venomous rays range in weight from less than a pound to hundreds of pounds and are widespread throughout the world. Rays inflict venomous painful wounds by means of a sharp spine on the tail, driven into the victim by a lashing movement of the tail. Rays do not attack man. Stingings usually result from stepping upon them and are defensive in nature.

Stingrays are most frequently found resting on the bottom, partially buried in the sand. Detection is often difficult. Wounds cause almost immediate intense pain with subsequent swelling, and although serious systemic effects are not common, several

Stingray.

fatalities have resulted from stings by very large rays.

Contact of a foot or other object with the dorsal surface of a ray usually results in a rapid lash of the tail with the sharp barb held erected so that it can be forced into the threatening object.

The spine is covered by a layer of tissue which tears easily during entry into the flesh, and the underlying venom is left in the wound after withdrawal.

The sharp barbs along the shaft of a stingray spine produce the lacerated type of wound often seen, although a puncture wound may occur. Immersion of the affected foot in very hot water quickly alleviates the pain.

Stings are most apt to occur if a person *runs* in the water, as a result of stepping directly upon a ray lying on the bottom. Rays tend to move away if one shuffles the feet along the sand.

Sea Snakes

A third group of venomous vertebrates are the sea snakes, various species of which are found in the tropical Indo-Pacific. The yellow-bellied sea snake is an example.

The tail is paddle-shaped, and its movements are very effective in propelling the animal through the water.

Although these air-breathing animals are relatively nonaggressive, bites do occur, and the venom is highly toxic. Early symptoms of poisoning are muscle pain and stiffness, which may be followed by muscle weakness. Death may occur as a result of respiratory failure, renal kidney failure, or other causes.

Bristle Worms

Among the marine invertebrates, certain annelid worms found in the sea and known as "bristle worms" or "fire worms" possess tufts of bristlelike structures called setae along their bodies. Contact with those bristles may result in a somewhat painful wound. It is not known if this response is due to a venom or simply to mechanical injury as a result of the bristles breaking off and penetrating the skin.

In some species the bristles are exceptionally long and cover almost the entire upper surface of the animal. They are present in tufts on both sides of each segment of the worm.

Glycera

Another type of worm, such as the bloodworm, Glycera, possesses biting jaws. The worm is commonly eight to ten inches long and at intervals everts its snout with its four sharp curved terminal jaws, which are black. Wounds may be quite painful and there is some indication that a venom may be present.

Jellyfishes

Another general group of venomous invertebrates are the coelenterates. A great variety of these interesting animals exists throughout the world.

The jellyfishes move by rhythmic contractions of the bell-shaped body. The tentacles and some other parts are armed with specialized stinging capsules known as nematocysts, which range in size from five to fifty or more microns.

Seen microscopically, the nematocysts of coelenterates appear as capsules with a long hollow threadlike tube coiled up inside. Contact with a tentacle can cause an almost explosive eversion of large numbers of these tubes and release of the venom within the capsules.

The extended thread may be several hundred times as long as the undischarged nematocysts and may have numerous barbs by which it becomes attached to the skin.

The thread is believed to turn inside out as it emerges from the capsule.

The effect of coelenterate stings in man due to discharge of venom from the nematocysts is highly variable. Local symptoms range from relatively mild skin irritation to severe pain and welts. Contact with the tentacles in some cases has caused marked systemic effects, and deaths have been reported following stings by some species.

Stings can also result from contact with the tentacles of dead specimens washed up on the beach.

The animals vary greatly in appearance and size, and the bell of some species may have a diameter as great as six feet, with tentacles trailing downward for perhaps a hundred feet.

Lion's Mane

Like other representatives of this class of coelenterates, the lion's mane captures animals that blunder into the mass of tentacles and are stung by the venom-containing nematocysts.

A fish may be captured after only slight contact with the tentacles and held tightly in spite of vigorous struggling. As the venom exerts its effect, the victim is eventually subdued and eaten.

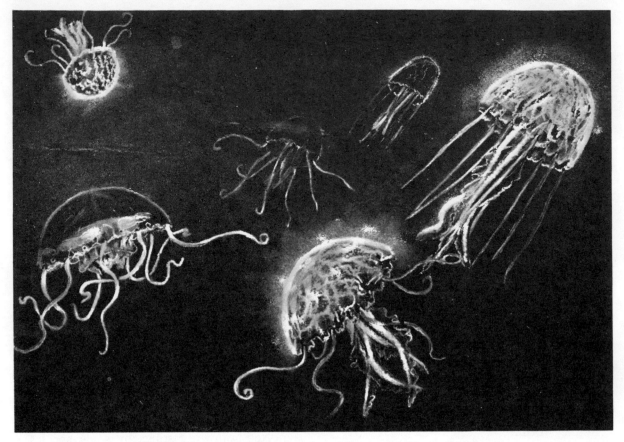

Jellyfish. Courtesy of the American Museum of Natural History

Portuguese Man-of-war

The Portuguese man-of-war is another type of coelenterate possessing nematocyst-bearing tentacles which may trail fifty or more feet below the float.

The float is a gas-filled bag, and the pressure of the wind upon the sail-like crest of this structure causes the animal to move slowly through the water. In contrast to the jellyfishes, movement of the man-of-war is controlled only by the wind and the ocean currents.

Man-of-war stings are not uncommon in some areas. Severe burning pain and local weal formation are the most common effects produced. Some individuals experience nausea, respiratory difficulty, and other systemic symptoms, but available data do not support the popular view that man-of-war stings are often fatal.

Persons touching the tentacles of dead specimens may also be stung. Fish and other animals may be captured after contact with a tentacle, and soon subdued and eaten.

The long tentacles have a beaded appearance due to the presence of batteries of nematocysts. They shorten and lengthen periodically, and the muscular elements can contract and bring captured prey up to the region of the digestive structures.

Hydroids

Hydroids, which are often found attached to rocks or other objects, may also cause painful stings. The tentacles possess the nematocysts characteristic of coelenterates.

Stinging Coral

The stinging or fire coral found in warm waters is another coelenterate which can cause a painful sting. Not a true coral, it is in the same animal class as the Portuguese man-of-war and the hydroids. It exists in a great variety of shapes ranging from upright columnar or fanlike structures to incrustations on rocks and other objects. The hard calcareous external skeleton is laid down by the innumerable individual polyps making up the colony.

If one brushes up against living fire coral with its multitude of tiny polyps, an almost immediate burning, stinging pain is produced by the venom of the discharged nematocysts.

The true corals, in contrast to the stinging corals, do not in general produce venomous wounds in man, although, of course, they can cause severe cuts.

Sea anemone. Courtesy of the American Museum of Natural History

Sea urchins and stinging (fire) coral. Courtesy University of California, Scripps Institution of Oceanography. Photo Willard Bascom

Anemones

Sea anemones also capture small animals by means of nematocysts. The small anemone fish is exceptional in that it lives in close association with certain anemones and is not stung; on the contrary it serves to attract larger fish into the anemone's grasp. If other fish brush up against the tentacles of these coelenterates, however, they may be captured and eaten.

If a person touches the tentacles of most sea anemones, the finger may become stuck lightly, but usually no symptoms are produced. Certain tropical anemones, however, can cause quite a painful sting.

Fish which touch even slightly one of the extended tentacles may be captured. After the initial capture, additional tentacles are then brought into action and escape becomes almost impossible.

Struggling may continue as the fish is drawn into the mouth of its captor.

The fish is finally consumed and digested in the internal cavity of the anemone.

Starfish. Courtesy of the American Museum of Natural History

Sea Urchins

Another general group of animals, of which some are venomous, are the echinoderms, comprising, among others, the sea urchins and starfishes. Certain warm-water sea urchins possess venomous spines which may puncture the flesh and cause an extremely painful wound.

The animals move about by means of the spines and also the tube feet which attach to rocks and other objects.

Many species of urchins are found throughout the world, but only a few appear to be capable of inflicting a venomous wound. Venomous sea urchins possess both long primary and shorter, thinner secondary spines. Only the thin spines are believed to possess a venom. Symptoms produced in man are local pain with variable amount of swelling.

Some short-spined sea urchins possess quite a different type of venom apparatus— small grasping organs known as pedicellariae which range in diameter from a fraction of a millimeter to several millimeters.

Cone shell. Courtesy of the American Museum of Natural History

Starfish

Another type of echinoderm is the starfish, most species of which are not venomous. However, certain species with stout spines may be capable of inflicting a venomous wound, although this has not been clearly established.

Contact with the spines has been reported to cause painful wounds but nothing is known about the nature of any venom.

Octopus

Certain mollusks are also venomous. The salivary secretions of the octopus contain toxic substances believed to be of impor-

tance in the capture of prey. Bites in humans by most species do not cause symptoms other than those due to the trauma produced by the animal's sharp beak. Some species, however, may cause severe local pain, swelling, and sometimes systemic effects.

Cone Shells

Some of the most interesting of the venomous marine animals are the mollusks of the genus conus, known commonly as the cone shells. These animals, found throughout much of the world, possess a unique and highly developed venom apparatus. Stings produce effects ranging from local pain to paralysis and death.

The animal usually withdraws into its shell when picked up but may occasionally sting a person if handled carelessly.

Following contact of the tip of the thin reddish orange snout, a hollow dartlike radula tooth is discharged into the flesh, and venom is injected through the lumen of the tooth. The prey of these gastropods are other snails, small fish, or various worms.

PHYSICAL DIVING HAZARDS

It is axiomatic that water constantly seeks its own level. The only rub is that it never finds it. Even the smallest body of water never rests. It is always in some degree of motion, due among other things to the speed and rotation of the earth and the magnetic attraction of the moon and sun. The effect of these forces varies directly with the size of the body of water, producing tides in oceans and slighter motions in smaller bodies of water. Added to these is the awesome force of the unhampered winds. These forces are transmitted to water, which is eight hundred times denser than air. Nothing in water can withstand its movement in currents, tides, and waves, and that includes you, for by comparison to the forces involved, you are nothing but an overgrown grain of sand on the beach.

When dealing with forces of such magnitude, one has little choice but to "swim with the current," and a diver should never forget this. To fight against such odds is to invite exhaustion and disaster. In relatively still bodies of water, surface currents are generated almost entirely by the wind. The results are surface waves, chop, or swells. When wind and water are moving together, the force of the wind is combined with the force of the moving water. Together, they can move a diver much farther than he can swim in the same amount of time. Or they can crush him against the shore with devastating effect.

When working against each other, their forces tend to cancel each other out, but the two are rarely, if ever, in perfect balance.

Therefore, you should learn to cope with these forces and use them to your own advantage. How do you learn? Experience is the only teacher, but perhaps I can warn you about what to expect.

Tidal Currents

The oceans slosh back and forth in their basins every six hours like clockwork, as a result, primarily, of the gravitational pull of the moon. In the process, as the water piles up on one shore it recedes from the opposite shore, in what are called high (flood) tides and low (ebb) tides. As the tides encounter the narrow passages that separate the many bays, inlets, harbors, or estuaries from the open sea, a *venturi* effect is created and the flow of water becomes much more extreme than normal. Bottom contours such as shoals and reefs can effect the same results. Thus there are always certain spots where divers simply should not dive except at brief periods between tides (that is, diving slack tides), and then only if necessary. These places and periods can easily be determined by consulting local experts or local charts and tide tables, which can be obtained at most boat marinas or from the U. S. Coast and Geodetic Survey in Washington, D.C.

If you are caught in an adverse current, swim diagonally with it to the closest shore point, even if it is not the one you want. Better a long walk than being swept out to sea. If the shore point is close enough and speed is essential to avoid missing it, swim diagonally against the current but anticipate the exhausting effort that will be required and pace yourself accordingly. If you are swept out to sea, don't panic. Inflate your life vest and float with it until the current turns and dissipates; you then can summon help or hop on your float and paddle ashore.

Surf Undertow

Seawater that continuously rolls ashore from the sea must return offshore to the sea, or our lands would soon be flooded. On sloping beaches the surface waves pile up relentlessly until they finally crest and topple over onto themselves in the form of surf. The water seeks the easiest return route to the sea, which is close to the bottom. The "bottom current" thus created is called undertow. It can be extremely strong, especially close to shore. If a strong wind is blowing parallel to shore or if there is a rip current present, the undertow may not run directly offshore but diagonally off in the direction of the wind or rip current. All undertows are very easy to avoid, however. All you need to do is stay on the surface.

Surf Breakers

All breakers are not of equal magnitude. The return flow of a particularly big wave tends to flatten out succeeding waves. Therefore only every third to seventh breaker is a really big one. When entering the water through surf, you should time your entry to begin just after a big breaker begins to wash offshore and go with it. When succeeding breakers approach, go to the bottom and let them roll over you, until you are beyond them.

When returning ashore through surf, good timing is essential. If the surf is light, you can pick a wave and ride it in. Then try to make it to the beach before the next wave breaks. If the surf is heavy or you are wearing heavy tanks, stay near the bottom as you ap-

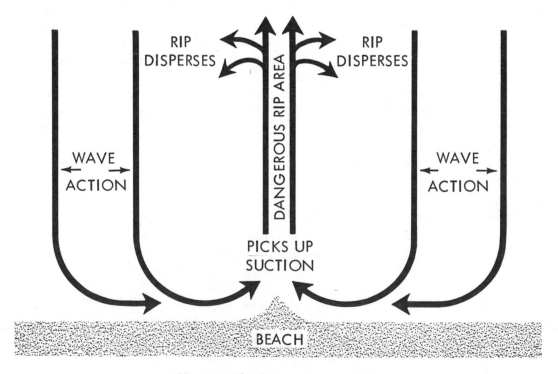

How rip tides (currents) are made.

proach shore, hanging on to something solid if possible during the backwash. When the water becomes so shallow that you cannot avoid the breakers, choose a nice one and let it take you in. Then get high and dry before the next one hits.

If you are wearing fins, enter and exit the surf walking backward, so that the fin blades won't buckle under and trip you. If you have a float, tow it behind you on entering and let it tow you on leaving. In both cases be sure all loose equipment is securely fastened.

Approaching a rocky shore in surf requires special skill and caution. If possible, exit in the lee of a shallow cove or big rock. As you approach your chosen point of exit, face the breakers (not the shore) and swim through or dive under the breakers until you see one that suits your taste. Then turn and pick out your foothold or handhold underwater as the breaker carries you in. Grab it, hold fast until the breaker recedes and then scramble ashore before the succeeding breaker gets to you. And good luck!

Rip Currents (Rip Tides)

Rip currents are caused by surf rolling over a shallow sandbar or reef into a lagoonlike basin and then exiting through widely separated channels that it cuts through the reef or bar as it escapes seaward. The rip current might run parallel to the shore until it reaches the channel, where it cuts sharply out to sea and then turns shoreward again.

Rip currents are usually so strong that they carry a heavy burden of silt or sand and tend to flatten out the breakers as they rush seaward. They can easily be detected by looking for the discolored water and flattened surf. If you get caught in a rip, swim at right angles to it. If it is carrying you seaward already, it is sometimes easier though less reassuring to let it carry you until it dissipates and turns shoreward again.

A similar kind of rip tide is caused when tides roll into a deep cove. The water rolls off the surrounding shores and returns seaward in the form of a rip current through the middle of the cove. Here again, swim cross current to shore or be swept out to sea. Always use a float or emergency flotation gear when diving where currents or rip currents are present.

Boats

When you are diving or snorkeling in popular boating areas, you always run the risk of being run over by a boat or injured by a whirling propeller. Avoid heavily trafficked areas and always display the "diver-down" flag. This is a red square with a white bar running diagonally from the upper staff corner to the lower free corner. Theoretically, at least, this warns boatmen to stay clear of the area because of the underwater activity. But take no chances. Always look and listen first, then surface with your hand or spear gun fully extended above your head. As for your own boat, stop the motor before allowing divers to enter or exit the water.

Spear Guns

Spear guns are lethal weapons and should always be treated with the respect due all firearms, whether ashore or underwater. Never point a loaded spear gun at anybody, no matter where you are. If your diving buddy carries a gun and you don't, let him lead. Always keep the trigger safety locked when stalking fish until you are ready to fire, and always fire or unload it before boating it. Then cover the barbed end with a large sheath or piece of cork, and set it out of the way and flat on the deck.

With experience, I think you will find that of all the dangerous creatures that frequent the sea, a careless man is by far the most dangerous.

Towering kelp like this has entangled divers on the West Coast. Photo Jack McKenney

Temperature

Water—especially the still water of lakes, ponds, quarries, and estuaries—stratifies itself into layers according to temperature. In summertime the bottom layers of water can be as much as 30 degrees colder than the surface layers. (In wintertime it is the reverse.) Therefore, know the character of the water before you dive. If you are going to need a diving suit, do not dive without one. It could only be a drudgery if you did, for nothing is more miserably uncomfortable than to get to the bottom on a long-planned dive only to begin trembling with the cold. Once shivering begins underwater, it is almost impossible to stop it until you return to the surface and restore your body warmth with a hot shower or a warm fire and hot liquids. Meanwhile, you exhaust yourself and overtax your heart.

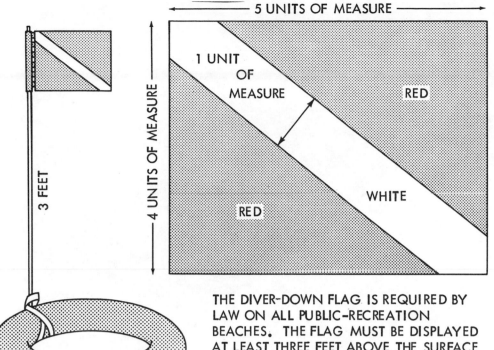

THE DIVER-DOWN FLAG IS REQUIRED BY
LAW ON ALL PUBLIC-RECREATION
BEACHES. THE FLAG MUST BE DISPLAYED
AT LEAST THREE FEET ABOVE THE SURFACE
FROM A BOAT AT ANCHOR WHEN DIVERS
ARE IN THE WATER OR ON THE FLOAT OF
DIVERS IN THE WATER.

"Diver-down" flag.

"Diver-down" flag on float. Photo Dave Woodford of Underwater Explorer's Club, Freeport, Grand Bahama, Courtesy Sports Creel

Diving under ice is dangerous and c-c-c-cold! U. S. Navy Photo

Your breathing pace triples and you consume most of your limited air supply in a futile but involuntary effort to produce enough heat to keep your body temperature up to normal. Furthermore, you become jittery and bumbling. You become dangerous to yourself and everyone near you. Worst of all, the joy is gone from diving. Insulated with a good wet suit, your body needs only a minute to warm the volume of trapped water before you can venture into even the coldest depths with great pleasure and relative comfort.

Chapter 7

UNDERWATER COMMUNICATIONS

Few sounds can be heard by divers underwater as we hear them on land, and audio communications between submerged divers are virtually impossible. The diver's ability to articulate underwater is sharply limited by the fact that he must hold a snorkel or breathing regulator clenched between his teeth, and since sound travels at 4900 feet per second underwater, whatever sounds can be heard are almost totally nondirectional. Thousands of dollars and man hours have been spent in various efforts to overcome these disadvantages—mostly on attempts to develop an electronically amplified voice communications system. However, a device that might give practical results with standard scuba gear remains in the realm of the improbable. Most scuba divers must rely solely on the old tried and true media of underwater communications: visual and line-pull signals. But even these have their limitations.

In my *Complete Illustrated Guide to Snorkel and Deep Diving* I pictorially presented the complete system of visual hand signals developed by Dr. Peter Wisher at Gallaudet College in Washington, D.C. If properly learned and practiced, this visual hand language would enable you to recite Shakespeare underwater. Yet I doubt that a single diver has bothered to commit it to memory since its publication—and understandably so. Like the tango, it takes two to communicate, and unless both are equally adept in the use of the medium, the chances are that communication will be slim, if not nil. I guess that asking divers to learn what amounts to a second language was just too much to ask two people to master. Therefore, improvisation remains the rule. You are left little choice but to improvise some basic kind of visual sign language with your diving buddy before each dive or else adjust to the idea that you are going to be practically incommunicado while underwater. If you dive often enough with the same diving buddy, you will find that your own private sign language will evolve of its own accord. Indeed, enough individuals have dived often enough with enough other individuals for a kind of basic visual communication system to have evolved on the national, if not the international, level. I have photographed those signs that I know are widely understood.

BASIC VISUAL HAND SIGNALS

Attention!
(Bang tank with knife.)

Out of air.

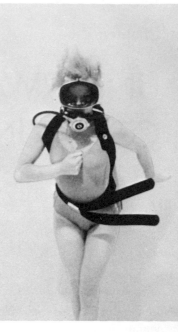

Low on air.

Going up.

"I don't understand."

"Okay."

BASIC VISUAL HAND SIGNALS

Concerning depth, time, or direction.

"This way."

"Help!"

"Stop."

BASIC VISUAL HAND SIGNALS

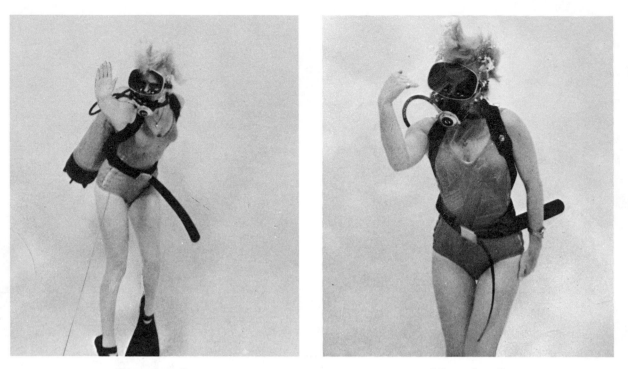

"Stay there."   "Come here."

*Jerry Conner, president of Kitch-
ener-Waterloo Dolphins' Club of
Canada, tests new electronic underwater communications device.
Photo Jack McKenney*

BASIC LINE PULL SIGNALS

ASCENT AND DESCENT (CODE: 4–2 PULLS)

Tender to Diver		Diver to Tender	
1 pull	OK?	1 pull	OK! Proceed.
2 pulls	Going down or stop and redescend.	2 pulls	Lower away or give slack.
3 pulls	Stop. Stand by to come up.	3 pulls	Stop. Take up slack.
4 pulls	Come up.	4 pulls	Take up.
2-1 pulls	I understand but wait a minute.	2-1 pulls	I understand but wait a minute.

SEARCHING (CODE: 7 PULLS)

1 pull	Stop and search there.	1 pull	I am stopping and searching here.
2 pulls	Follow where the life line leads you or (if using circle search) circle around.	2 pulls	I am following the line (diver must keep line taut) or circling.
3 pulls	Move to right.	3 pulls	I am moving to my right.
4 pulls	Move to left.	4 pulls	I am moving to my left.
5 pulls	You are there.	5 pulls	I have found objective.

EMERGENCY SIGNALS (NO CODE)

2-2-2 pulls	(Answer only.) I acknowledge you are fouled and need assistance.	2-2-2 pulls	I am fouled and need assistance from a diver.
3-3-3 pulls	I acknowledge you are fouled but are safe.	3-3-3 pulls	I am fouled but can clear myself.
4-4-4 pulls	Come up immediately!	4-4-4 pulls	Haul me up immediately!

LIFTING AND LOWERING (CODE: 2–4 PULLS)

1 pull	Stop.	1 pull	Stop.
2 pulls	Slack off.	2 pulls	Slack off.
3 pulls	Take up slack.	3 pulls	Take up slack.
4 pulls	Haul away.	4 pulls	Haul away.
5 pulls	Line coming.	5 pulls	Send me a line.

Devise your own sign language if all else fails. Photo Chuck Irwin

Chapter 8

U.S. NAVY DECOMPRESSION TABLES AND RELATED DATA

GENERAL

The tables and procedures outlined herein have been developed to provide safety from the hazards of decompression sickness. At the same time, the tables have been made as efficient as possible in order that they will be the least possible hindrance to diving operations.

AIR DECOMPRESSION TABLES

GENERAL

(1) The air decompression tables comprise:
   (*a*) Decompression Procedures (table 1–4, this page).
   (*b*) U. S. Navy Standard Air Decompression Table (table 1–5, page 112).
   (*c*) "No Decompression Limits and Repetitive Groups" (table 1–6, page 113).
   (*d*) Surface Interval Credit Table (table 1–7, page 115).
   (*e*) Repetitive Dive Timetable (table 1–8, page 116).
   (*f*) Standard Air Decompression Table for Exceptional Exposures (table 1–9, page 117).
(2) Regardless of the type of diving apparatus, for all dives where air is the breathing medium, use these tables as prescribed.

Table 1–4.—Decompression procedures.

GENERAL INSTRUCTIONS FOR AIR DIVING

NEED FOR DECOMPRESSION

A quantity of nitrogen is taken up by the body during every dive. The amount absorbed depends upon the depth of the dive and the exposure (bottom) time. If the quantity of nitrogen dissolved in the body tissues exceeds a certain critical amount, the ascent must be delayed to allow the body tissue to remove the excess nitrogen. Decompression sickness results from failure to delay the ascent and to allow this process of gradual desaturation. A specified time at a specific depth for purposes of desaturation is called a decompression stop.

"NO DECOMPRESSION" SCHEDULES

Dives that are not long or deep enough to require decompression stops are "no decompression" dives. Dives to 33 feet or less do not require decompression stops. As the depth increases, the allowable bottom time for "no decompression" dives decreases. Five minutes at 190 feet is the shortest and deepest "no decompression" schedule. These dives are all listed in the *No Decompression Limits and Repetitive Group Designation Table for "No Decompression" Dives, "No Decompression Table"* (table 1–6) and only require compliance with the 60 feet per minute rate of ascent.

Schedules That Require Decompression Stops

All dives beyond the limits of the *"No Decompression Table"* require decompression stops. These dives are listed in the *Navy Standard Air Decompression*

Table (table 1–5). Comply exactly with instructions except as modified by surface decompression procedures.

VARIATIONS IN RATE OF ASCENT

Ascend from all dives at the rate of 60 feet per minute.

In the event you exceed the 60 feet per minute rate:

(1) If no decompression stops are required, but the bottom time places you within 10 minutes of a schedule that does require decompression; stop at 10 feet for the time that you should have taken in ascent at 60 feet per minute.

(2) If decompression is required; stop 10 feet below the first listed decompression depth for the time that you should have taken in ascent at 60 feet per minute.

In the event you are unable to maintain the 60 feet per minute rate of ascent:

(1) If the delay was at or near the bottom; add to the bottom time, the additional time used in ascent. Decompress according to the requirements of the total bottom time. This is the safer procedure.

(2) If the delay was near the surface; increase the first stop by the difference between the time consumed in ascent and the time that should have been consumed at 60 feet per minute.

REPETITIVE DIVE PROCEDURE

A dive performed within 12 hours of surfacing from a previous dive is a repetitive dive. The period between dives is the surface interval. Excess nitrogen requires 12 hours to effectively be lost from the body. These tables are designed to protect the diver from the effects of this residual nitrogen. Allow a minimum surface interval of 10 minutes between all dives. Specific instructions are given for the use of each table in the following order:

(1) The *"No Decompression Table"* or the *Navy Standard Air Decompression Table* gives the repetitive group designation for all schedules which may precede a repetitive dive.

(2) The *Surface Interval Credit Table* gives credit for the desaturation occurring during the surface interval.

(3) The *Repetitive Dive Timetable* gives the number of minutes or residual nitrogen time to add to the actual bottom time of the repetitive dive in order to obtain decompression for the residual nitrogen.

(4) The *"No Decompression Table"* or the *Navy Standard Air Decompression Table* gives the decompression required for the repetitive dive.

U. S. NAVY STANDARD AIR DECOMPRESSION TABLE

INSTRUCTIONS FOR USE

Time of decompression stops in the table is in minutes.

Enter the table at the exact or the next greater depth than the maximum depth attained during the dive. Select the listed bottom time that is exactly equal to or is next greater than the bottom time of the dive. Maintain the diver's chest as close as possible to each decompression depth for the number of minutes listed. The rate of ascent *between* stops is not critical. Commence timing each stop on arrival at the decompression depth and resume ascent when the specified time has lapsed.

For example—a dive to 82 feet for 36 minutes. To determine the proper decompression procedure: The next greater depth listed in this table is 90 feet. The next greater bottom time listed opposite 90 feet is 40. Stop 7 minutes at 10 feet in accordance with the 90/40 schedule.

For example—a dive to 110 feet for 30 minutes. It is known that the depth did not exceed 110 feet. To determine the proper decompression schedule: The exact depth of 110 feet is listed. The exact bottom time of 30 minutes is listed opposite 110 feet. Decompress according to the 110/30 schedule unless the dive was particularly cold or arduous. In that case, go to the 110/40, the 120/30, or the 120/40 at your own discretion.

(End of Table 1–4.)

SINGLE DIVES

(3) A single dive is the first dive of the day. It is denoted by an exposure to a specific depth in feet for a specific time in minutes. An example would be 134 feet for 14 minutes. The depth is the maximum depth attained. The time is the actual bottom time. Bottom time is the elapsed time between leaving the surface in descent and leaving the deepest depth in ascent. A combination of depth and time listed in the decompression tables is called a dive schedule. All dives are included and covered in the next deeper and next longer schedule. Do not interpolate.

REPETITIVE DIVES

(4) Any dive performed within 12 hours of a previous dive is a *repetitive dive*. The period between dives is the *surface interval*. Decompression following a repetitive dive requires special consideration. This is because dissolved inert gas from the previous dive remains in the body at the *beginning* of the repetitive dive.

(5) A detailed consideration of all the factors involved would be prohibitively complicated. A simplified and workable solution is based on the degree of saturation of the "120 minute half-time tissue." The basic idea of this approach involves considering the previous dive, the surface interval, and the repetitive dive together as a whole to yield an *equivalent single dive*. For the *depth* of the equivalent single dive, the *actual* depth of the repetitive dive is used. But the *bottom time* is the sum of the actual time plus an additional amount of time to take into account the residual nitrogen from the previous dive and surface interval.

(6) Upon surfacing from a dive, the diver is catalogued by table 1–5 or 1–6 into one of 16 lettered *repetitive groups* in accordance with the amount of inert gas left in his body. During the surface interval the diver loses inert gas and is given "credit" for the loss by means of table 1–7, which shows the change from one group to another for various time intervals on the surface. For every depth of dive, there is a certain time of exposure that would bring the diver to the same degree of saturation as that represented by each repetitive group. This time, based on the residual inert gas from previous dive and surface interval, is called the *residual nitrogen time*. In table 1–8, residual nitrogen time is expressed as a number of minutes for various depths (in 10-foot increments) and for each repetitive group designation. The bottom time of the *equivalent single dive* is then obtained by adding this residual nitrogen time to the actual bottom time of the repetitive dive being considered. The proper decompression for the ascent from the repetitive dive may then be found in the Standard Air Decompression Table (table 1–5) by using the actual depth of the repetitive dive and the equivalent single dive bottom time. Successive repetitive dives may be handled similarly.

(7) The Standard Air Decompression Table (table 1–5) covers the normal range of diving. The depth limit is 190 feet and the bottom time limit for each depth is approximately 12,000 divided by the depth. This is an arbitrary time, but it is a good maximum for normal practice. Stay within the limits of this table for all routine air dives.

(8) Details on the use of the Standard Air Decompression Tables are:

(*a*) Time of decompression stops in the table is in minutes.

(*b*) Enter the tables at the listed depth that is exactly equal to or is the next greater than the maximum attained during the dive.

(*c*) Select the bottom time listed for the selected depth that is exactly equal or is next greater than the bottom time of the dive.

(*d*) Use the decompression stops listed on the line for the selected bottom time.

(*e*) For any repetitive diving, use the repetitive group designation listed on the same line (or if no decompression is required, obtain the repetitive group from table 1–6).

(*f*) Maintain the diver's *chest* as close as possible to each decompression depth for the number of minutes listed.

(*g*) The rate of ascent *between* stops is not critical. Commence timing each stop on arrival at the decompression depth and resume ascent when the specified time has elapsed.

(9) Specific examples of the use of the table are:

(*a*) You made a single dive to 82 feet for 36 minutes. You wish to determine the proper decompression procedure:

DEPTH (ft.)	BOT-TOM TIME (min.)	TIME TO FIRST STOP	50	40	30	20	10	TOTAL ASCENT TIME	REPET. GROUP
40	200						0	0.7	*
	210	0.5					2	2.5	N
	230	0.5					7	7.5	N
	250	0.5					11	11.5	O
	270	0.5					15	15.5	O
	300	0.5					19	19.5	Z
50	100						0	0.8	*
	110	0.7					3	3.7	L
	120	0.7					5	5.7	M
	140	0.7					10	10.7	M
	160	0.7					21	21.7	N
	180	0.7					29	29.7	O
	200	0.7					35	35.7	O
	220	0.7					40	40.7	Z
	240	0.7					47	47.7	Z
60	60						0	1.0	*
	70	0.8					2	2.8	K
	80	0.8					7	7.8	L
	100	0.8					14	14.8	M
	120	0.8					26	26.8	N
	140	0.8					39	39.8	O
	160	0.8					48	48.8	Z
	180	0.8					56	56.8	Z
	200	0.6				1	69	70.6	Z
70	50						0	1.2	*
	60	1.0					8	9.0	K
	70	1.0					14	15.0	L
	80	1.0					18	19.0	M
	90	1.0					23	24.0	N
	100	1.0					33	34.0	N
	110	0.8				2	41	43.8	O
	120	0.8				4	47	51.8	O
	130	0.8				6	52	58.8	O
	140	0.8				8	56	64.8	Z
	150	0.8				9	61	70.8	Z
	160	0.8				13	72	85.8	Z
	170	0.8				19	79	98.8	Z
80	40						0	1.3	*
	50	1.2					10	11.2	K
	60	1.2					17	18.2	L
	70	1.2					23	24.2	M
	80	1.0				2	31	34.0	N
	90	1.0				7	39	47.0	N
	100	1.0				11	46	58.0	O
	110	1.0				13	53	67.0	O
	120	1.0				17	56	74.0	Z
	130	1.0				19	63	83.0	Z
	140	1.0				26	69	96.0	Z
	150	1.0				32	77	110.0	Z
90	30						0	1.5	*
	40	1.3					7	8.3	J
	50	1.3					18	19.3	L
	60	1.3					25	26.3	M
	70	1.2				7	30	38.2	N
	80	1.2				13	40	54.2	N
	90	1.2				18	48	67.2	O
	100	1.2				21	54	76.2	Z
	110	1.2				24	61	86.2	Z
	120	1.2				32	68	101.2	Z
	130	1.0			5	36	74	116.0	Z
100	25						0	1.7	*
	30	1.5					3	4.5	I
	40	1.5					15	16.5	K
	50	1.3				2	24	27.3	L
	60	1.3				9	28	38.3	N
	70	1.3				17	39	57.3	O
	80	1.3				23	48	72.3	O
	90	1.2			3	23	57	84.2	Z
	100	1.2			7	23	66	97.2	Z
	110	1.2			10	34	72	117.2	Z
	120	1.2			12	41	78	132.2	Z
110	20						0	1.8	*
	25	1.7					3	4.7	H
	30	1.7					7	8.7	J
	40	1.5				2	21	24.5	L
	50	1.5				8	26	35.5	M
	60	1.5				18	36	55.5	N
	70	1.3			1	23	48	73.3	O
	80	1.3			7	23	57	88.3	Z
	90	1.3			12	30	64	107.3	Z
	100	1.3			15	37	72	125.3	Z

DEPTH (ft.)	BOT-TOM TIME (min.)	TIME TO FIRST STOP	50	40	30	20	10	TOTAL ASCENT TIME	REPET. GROUP
120	15						0	2.0	*
	20	1.8					2	3.8	H
	25	1.8					6	7.8	I
	30	1.8					14	15.8	J
	40	1.7				5	25	31.7	L
	50	1.7				15	31	47.7	N
	60	1.5			2	22	45	70.5	O
	70	1.5			9	23	55	88.5	O
	80	1.5			15	27	63	106.5	Z
	90	1.5			19	37	74	131.5	Z
	100	1.5			23	45	80	149.5	Z
130	10						0	2.2	*
	15	2.0					1	3.0	F
	20	2.0					4	6.0	H
	25	2.0					10	12.0	J
	30	1.8				3	18	22.8	M
	40	1.8				10	25	36.8	N
	50	1.7			3	21	37	62.7	O
	60	1.7			9	23	52	85.7	Z
	70	1.7			16	24	61	102.7	Z
	80	1.5		3	19	35	72	130.5	Z
	90	1.5		8	19	45	80	153.5	Z
140	10						0	2.3	*
	15	2.2					2	4.2	G
	20	2.2					6	8.2	I
	25	2.0				2	14	18.0	J
	30	2.0				5	21	28.0	K
	40	1.8			2	16	26	45.8	N
	50	1.8			6	24	44	75.8	O
	60	1.8			16	23	56	96.8	Z
	70	1.7		4	19	32	68	124.7	Z
	80	1.7		10	23	41	79	154.7	Z
150	5						0	2.5	C
	10	2.3					1	3.3	E
	15	2.3					3	5.3	G
	20	2.2				2	7	11.2	H
	25	2.2				4	17	23.2	K
	30	2.2				8	24	34.2	L
	40	2.0			5	19	33	59.0	N
	50	2.0			12	23	51	88.0	O
	60	1.8		3	19	26	62	111.8	Z
	70	1.8		11	19	39	75	145.8	Z
	80	1.7	1	17	19	50	84	172.7	Z
160	5						0	2.7	D
	10	2.5					1	3.5	F
	15	2.3				1	4	7.3	H
	20	2.3				3	11	16.3	J
	25	2.3				7	20	29.3	K
	30	2.2			2	11	25	40.2	M
	40	2.2			7	23	39	71.2	N
	50	2.0		2	16	23	55	98.0	Z
	60	2.0		9	19	33	69	132.0	Z
	70	1.8	1	17	22	44	80	165.8	Z
170	5						0	2.8	D
	10	2.7					2	4.7	F
	15	2.5				2	5	9.5	H
	20	2.5				4	15	21.5	J
	25	2.3			2	7	23	34.3	L
	30	2.3			4	13	26	45.3	M
	40	2.2		1	10	23	45	81.2	O
	50	2.2		5	18	23	61	109.2	Z
	60	2.0	2	15	22	37	74	152.0	Z
	70	2.0	8	17	19	51	86	183.0	Z
180	5						0	3.0	D
	10	2.8					3	5.8	F
	15	2.7				3	6	11.7	I
	20	2.5			1	5	17	25.5	K
	25	2.5			3	10	24	39.5	L
	30	2.5			6	17	27	52.5	N
	40	2.3		3	14	23	50	92.3	O
	50	2.2	2	9	19	30	65	127.2	Z
	60	2.2	5	16	19	44	81	167.2	Z
190	5						0	3.2	D
	10	2.8				1	3	6.8	G
	15	2.8				4	7	13.8	I
	20	2.7			2	6	20	30.7	K
	25	2.7			5	11	25	43.7	M
	30	2.5		1	8	19	32	62.5	N
	40	2.5		8	14	23	55	102.5	O
	50	2.3	4	13	22	33	72	146.3	Z
	60	2.3	10	17	19	50	84	182.3	Z

*See table 1-6 for repetitive groups in "no decompression" dives.

Table 1–5.—U. S. Navy standard air decompression table.

DEPTH (ft.)	NO DECOMPRESSION LIMITS (Min.)	REPETITIVE GROUPS														
		A	B	C	D	E	F	G	H	I	J	K	L	M	N	O
10	—	60	120	210	300											
15	—	35	70	110	160	225	350									
20	—	25	50	75	100	135	180	240	325							
25	—	20	35	55	75	100	125	160	195	245	315					
30	—	15	30	45	60	75	95	120	145	170	205	250	310			
35	310	5	15	25	40	50	60	80	100	120	140	160	190	220	270	310
40	200	5	15	25	30	40	50	70	80	100	110	130	150	170	200	
50	100	—	10	15	25	30	40	50	60	70	80	90	100			
60	60	—	10	15	20	25	30	40	50	55	60					
70	50	—	5	10	15	20	30	35	40	45	50					
80	40	—	5	10	15	20	25	30	35	40						
90	30	—	5	10	12	15	20	25	30							
100	25	—	5	7	10	15	20	22	25							
110	20	—	—	5	10	13	15	20								
120	15	—	—	5	10	12	15									
130	10	—	—	5	8	10										
140	10	—	—	5	7	10										
150	5	—	—	5												
160	5	—	—	—	5											
170	5	—	—	—	5											
180	5	—	—	—	5											
190	5	—	—	—	5											

INSTRUCTIONS FOR USE

I. "No decompression" limits

This column shows at various depths greater than 30 feet the allowable diving times (in minutes) which permit surfacing directly at 60 ft. a minute with no decompression stops. Longer exposure times require the use of the Standard Air Decompression Table (Table 1-5).

II. Repetitive group designation table

The tabulated exposure times (or bottom times) are in minutes. The times at the various depths in each vertical column are the maximum exposures during which a diver will remain within the group listed at the head of the column.

To find the repetitive group designation at surfacing for dives involving exposures up to and including the "no decompression limits": Enter the table on the *exact or next greater depth* than that to which exposed and select the listed exposure time *exact or next greater* than the actual exposure time. The repetitive group designation is indicated by the letter at the head of the vertical column where the selected exposure time is listed.

For example: A dive was to 32 feet for 45 minutes. Enter the table along the 35 ft. depth line since it is next greater than 32 ft. The table shows that since group "D" is left after 40 minutes exposure and group "E" after 50 minutes, group "E" (at the head of the column where the 50 min. exposure is listed) is the proper selection.

Exposure times for depths less than 40 ft. are listed only up to approximately five hours since this is considered to be beyond field requirements for this table.

Table 1–6.—"No decompression" limits and repetitive group designation table for "no decompression" dives ("No Decompression Table").

The next greater depth listed in the table is 90 feet. The next greater bottom time listed opposite 90 feet is 40 minutes. The proper decompression procedure is therefore a 7-minute stop at 10 feet in accordance with 90/40 schedule.

(*b*) You made a single dive to 110 feet for 30 minutes. You know that the depth did not exceed 110 feet. You wish to determine the proper decompression procedure: The exact depth of 110 feet is listed. The exact time of 30 minutes is listed opposite 90 feet. Decompress according to the 110/30 schedule unless the dive was particularly cold or arduous or conditions will prohibit accurate decompression. In any of these cases go to the 110/40, the 120/30 or the 120/40 schedule at your own discretion.

(10) The "No Decompression Table" (table 1–6) is officially and more accurately titled *"No Decompression" Limits and Repetitive Group Designation Table for "No Decompression" Schedules*. It is a new table required by repetitive diving. It is no longer sufficient merely to know where decompression requirements begin. In repetitive diving you must know the amount of nitrogen remaining in the tissues from any dive, no matter how short or shallow. The repetitive group designations provide that information.

(11) Repetitive group designations are given for depths of 10 feet to 40 feet in 5-foot increments and for depths of 40 feet to 300 feet in 10-foot increments. Opposite each depth and each repetitive group is listed the maximum bottom time which will allow the diver to remain within the group. On the assumption that it is the operational limit, the times for 10 to 25 feet end at about 5 hours. From 40 feet on, the times end at the "no decompression" limit.

(12) The "no decompression" limits listed in this table for depths of 40 feet and greater are useful in planning operations. The diver may surface directly ("no decompression dive") as long as the bottom time is less than the maximum listed for the depth. For depths not greater than 33 feet, direct surfacing is permissible regardless of the bottom time.

(13) Other than the above uses to obtain "no decompression" limits, the only purpose of this table is to provide the repetitive group designation for "no decompression" dives. This knowledge is necessary to make repetitive dives after "no decompression" dives.

(14) Details and an example of its use to obtain the repetitive group designations are given directly on the table.

(15) The Surface Interval Credit Table is another requirement of the repetitive diving system. It is the real reason for the success and efficiency of the repetitive dive system.

(16) The diver continues to lose nitrogen while he is on the surface until he is completely desaturated. This requires 12 hours or more. In order to provide efficient decompression instructions, it is necessary to know the amount of nitrogen remaining in the tissues at the time a repetitive dive commences. This table provides that information.

(17) The repetitive groups are the measuring units. In this table, the loss of inert gas with increasing length of surface interval is reflected in the change from one group to another.

(18) Details and an example of its use are given directly on the table.

(19) The Repetitive Dive Timetable lists the number of minutes at each depth that will build up the nitrogen partial pressure represented by each repetitive group.

(20) Knowing the diver's repetitive group designation, the system gives an arbitrary bottom time (the residual nitrogen time) that he must assume he has already completed when he starts his repetitive dive. This arbitrary bottom time and the actual bottom time of the repetitive dive are added to yield the bot-

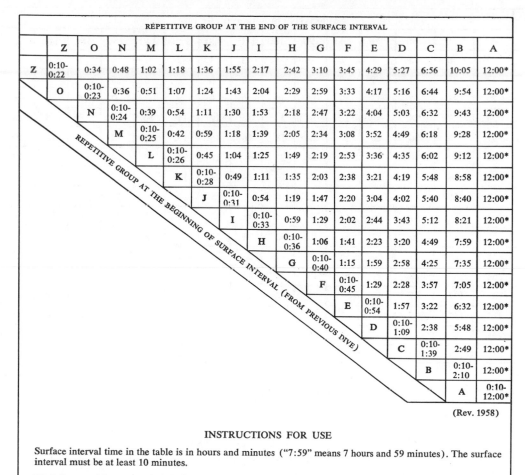

	Z	O	N	M	L	K	J	I	H	G	F	E	D	C	B	A
Z	0:10-0:22	0:34	0:48	1:02	1:18	1:36	1:55	2:17	2:42	3:10	3:45	4:29	5:27	6:56	10:05	12:00*
O		0:10-0:23	0:36	0:51	1:07	1:24	1:43	2:04	2:29	2:59	3:33	4:17	5:16	6:44	9:54	12:00*
N			0:10-0:24	0:39	0:54	1:11	1:30	1:53	2:18	2:47	3:22	4:04	5:03	6:32	9:43	12:00*
M				0:10-0:25	0:42	0:59	1:18	1:39	2:05	2:34	3:08	3:52	4:49	6:18	9:28	12:00*
L					0:10-0:26	0:45	1:04	1:25	1:49	2:19	2:53	3:36	4:35	6:02	9:12	12:00*
K						0:10-0:28	0:49	1:11	1:35	2:03	2:38	3:21	4:19	5:48	8:58	12:00*
J							0:10-0:31	0:54	1:19	1:47	2:20	3:04	4:02	5:40	8:40	12:00*
I								0:10-0:33	0:59	1:29	2:02	2:44	3:43	5:12	8:21	12:00*
H									0:10-0:36	1:06	1:41	2:23	3:20	4:49	7:59	12:00*
G										0:10-0:40	1:15	1:59	2:58	4:25	7:35	12:00*
F											0:10-0:45	1:29	2:28	3:57	7:05	12:00*
E												0:10-0:54	1:57	3:22	6:32	12:00*
D													0:10-1:09	2:38	5:48	12:00*
C														0:10-1:39	2:49	12:00*
B															0:10-2:10	12:00*
A																0:10-12:00*

Top banner: REPETITIVE GROUP AT THE END OF THE SURFACE INTERVAL

Diagonal label: REPETITIVE GROUP AT THE BEGINNING OF SURFACE INTERVAL (FROM PREVIOUS DIVE)

(Rev. 1958)

INSTRUCTIONS FOR USE

Surface interval time in the table is in hours and minutes ("7:59" means 7 hours and 59 minutes). The surface interval must be at least 10 minutes.

Find the repetitive group designation letter (from the previous dive schedule) on the diagonal slope. Enter the table horizontally to select the listed surface interval time that is exactly or next greater than the actual surface interval time. The repetitive group designation for the end of the surface interval is at the head of the vertical column where the selected surface interval time is listed. For example — a previous dive was to 110 ft. for 30 minutes. The diver remains on the surface 1 hour and 30 minutes and wishes to find the new repetitive group designation: The repetitive group from the last column of the 110/30 schedule in the Standard Air Decompression Tables is "J". Enter the surface interval credit table along the horizontal line labeled "J". The 1 hour and 47 min. listed surface interval time is next greater than the actual 1 hour and 30 minutes surface interval time. Therefore, the diver has lost sufficient inert gas to place him in group "G" (at the head of the vertical column selected).

*NOTE: Dives following surface intervals of more than 12 hours are not considered repetitive dives. Actual bottom times in the Standard Air Decompression Tables may be used in computing decompression for such dives.

Table 1–7.—Surface interval credit table.

tom time of the equivalent single dive mentioned previously.

(21) Details and an example of its use are given directly on the table.

(22) There is one exception to the table. It occasionally occurs when the repetitive dive is to the same or greater depth than the initial dives and the surface interval is short. Because of the necessity to account for the greatest exposure within a group, the arbitrary bottom time assigned may be greater than the sum of the actual bottom times of the previous dives. In such case, if the repetitive dive is to the same or greater depth than the previous

REPET. GROUPS	REPETITIVE DIVE DEPTH (Ft.)															
	40	50	60	70	80	90	100	110	120	130	140	150	160	170	180	190
A	7	6	5	4	4	3	3	3	3	3	2	2	2	2	2	2
B	17	13	11	9	8	7	7	6	6	6	5	5	4	4	4	4
C	25	21	17	15	13	11	10	10	9	8	7	7	6	6	6	6
D	37	29	24	20	18	16	14	13	12	11	10	9	9	8	8	8
E	49	38	30	26	23	20	18	16	15	13	12	12	11	10	10	10
F	61	47	36	31	28	24	22	20	18	16	15	14	13	13	12	11
G	73	56	44	37	32	29	26	24	21	19	18	17	16	15	14	13
H	87	66	52	43	38	33	30	27	25	22	20	19	18	17	16	15
I	101	76	61	50	43	38	34	31	28	25	23	22	20	19	18	17
J	116	87	70	57	48	43	38	34	32	28	26	24	23	22	20	19
K	138	99	79	64	54	47	43	38	35	31	29	27	26	24	22	21
L	161	111	88	72	61	53	48	42	39	35	32	30	28	26	25	24
M	187	124	97	80	68	58	52	47	43	38	35	32	31	29	27	26
N	213	142	107	87	73	64	57	51	46	40	38	35	33	31	29	28
O	241	160	117	96	80	70	62	55	50	44	40	38	36	34	31	30
Z	257	169	122	100	84	73	64	57	52	46	42	40	37	35	32	31

(Rev. 1958)

INSTRUCTIONS FOR USE

The bottom times listed in this table are called "residual nitrogen times" and are the times a diver is to consider he has *already* spent on bottom when he *starts* a repetitive dive to a specific depth. They are in minutes.

Enter the table horizontally with the repetitive group designation from the Surface Interval Credit Table. The time in each vertical column is the number of minutes that would be required (at the depth listed at the head of the column) to saturate to the particular group.

For example—the final group designation from the Surface Interval Credit Table, on the basis of a previous dive and surface interval, is "H". To plan a dive to 110 feet, determine the "residual nitrogen time" for this depth required by the repetitive group designation: Enter this table along the horizontal line labeled "H". The table shows that one must *start* a dive to 110 feet as though he had already been on the bottom for 27 minutes. This information can then be applied to the Standard Air Decompression table or "No Decompression" Table in a number of ways:

(1) Assuming a diver is going to finish a job and take whatever decompression is required, he must add 27 minutes to his actual bottom time and be prepared to take decompression according to the 110 foot schedules for the sum or equivalent single dive time.

(2) Assuming one wishes to make a quick inspection dive for the minimum decompression, he will decompress according to the 110/30 schedule for a dive of 3 minutes or less (27 + 3 = 30). For a dive of over 3 minutes but less than 13, he will decompress according to the 110/40 schedule (27 + 13 = 40).

(3) Assuming that one does not want to exceed the 110/50 schedule and the amount of decompression it requires, he will have to start ascent before 23 minutes of actual bottom time (50 − 27 = 23).

(4) Assuming that a diver has air for approximately 45 minutes bottom time and decompression stops, the possible dives can be computed: A dive of 13 minutes will require 23 minutes of decompression (110/40 schedule), for a total submerged time of 36 minutes. A dive of 13 to 23 minutes will require 34 minutes of decompression (110/50 schedule), for a total submerged time of 47 to 57 minutes. Therefore, to be safe, the diver will have to start ascent before 13 minutes or a standby air source will have to be provided.

Table 1–8.—Repetitive dive timetable.

Depth (ft.)	Bottom Time (Min.)	Time to First Stop	130	120	110	100	90	80	70	60	50	40	30	20	10	Total Ascent Time
40	360	0.5													23	24
	480	0.5													41	42
	720	0.5													69	70
60	240	0.7												2	79	82
	360	0.7												20	119	140
	480	0.7												44	148	193
	720	0.7												78	187	266
80	180	1.0												35	85	121
	240	0.8											6	52	120	179
	360	0.8											29	90	160	280
	480	0.8											59	107	187	354
	720	0.7										17	108	142	187	455
100	180	1.0										1	29	53	118	202
	240	1.0										14	42	84	142	283
	360	0.8									2	42	73	111	187	416
	480	0.8									21	61	91	142	187	502
	720	0.8									55	106	122	142	187	613
120	120	1.3										10	19	47	98	176
	180	1.2									5	27	37	76	137	283
	240	1.2									23	35	60	97	179	395
	360	1.0								18	45	64	93	142	187	550
	480	0.8							3	41	64	93	122	142	187	653
	720	0.8							32	74	100	114	122	142	187	772
140	90	1.5									2	14	18	42	88	166
	120	1.5									12	14	36	56	120	240
	180	1.3								10	26	32	54	94	168	386
	240	1.2							8	28	34	50	78	124	187	511
	360	1.0						9	32	42	64	84	122	142	187	683
	480	1.0						31	44	59	100	114	122	142	187	800
	720	0.8					16	56	88	97	100	114	122	142	187	923
170	90	1.8								12	12	14	34	52	120	232
	120	1.5						2	10	12	18	32	42	82	156	356
	180	1.3					4	10	22	28	34	50	78	120	187	535
	240	1.3					18	24	30	42	50	70	116	142	187	681
	360	1.2				22	34	40	52	60	98	114	122	142	187	873
	480	1.0			14	40	42	56	91	97	100	114	122	142	187	1006
200	5	3.2													1	5
	10	3.0												1	4	8
	15	2.8											1	4	10	18
	20	2.8											3	7	27	40
	25	2.8											7	14	25	49
	30	2.7										2	9	22	37	73
	40	2.5									2	8	17	23	59	112
	50	2.5									6	16	22	39	75	161
	60	2.3								2	13	17	24	51	89	199
	90	1.8					1	10	10	12	12	30	38	74	134	323
	120	1.7					6	10	10	24	28	40	64	98	180	472
	180	1.3		1	10	10	18	24	24	42	48	70	106	142	187	684
	240	1.3		6	20	24	24	36	42	54	68	114	122	142	187	841
	360	1.2	12	22	36	40	44	56	82	98	100	114	122	142	187	1057
210	5	3.3													1	5
	10	3.2												2	4	10
	15	3.0											1	5	13	22
	20	3.0											4	10	23	40
	25	2.8										2	7	17	27	56
	30	2.8										4	9	24	41	81
	40	2.7									4	9	19	26	63	124
	50	2.5								1	9	17	19	45	80	174
220	5	3.5													2	6
	10	3.3												2	5	11
	15	3.2											2	5	16	27
	20	3.0										1	3	11	24	43
	25	3.0										3	8	19	33	66
	30	2.8									1	7	10	23	47	91
	40	2.8									6	12	22	29	68	140
	50	2.7								3	12	17	18	51	86	190
230	5	3.7													2	6
	10	3.3											1	2	6	13
	15	3.3											3	6	18	31
	20	3.2										2	5	12	26	49
	25	3.2										4	8	22	37	75
	30	3.0									2	8	12	23	51	99
	40	2.8								1	7	15	22	34	74	156
	50	2.8								5	14	16	24	51	89	202
240	5	3.8													2	6
	10	3.5											1	3	6	14
	15	3.5											4	6	21	35
	20	3.3										3	6	15	25	53
	25	3.2									1	4	9	24	40	82
	30	3.2									2	8	15	22	56	109
	40	3.0								3	7	17	22	39	75	166
	50	2.8							1	8	15	16	29	51	94	217
250	5	3.8												1	2	7
	10	3.7											1	4	7	16
	15	3.5										1	4	7	22	38
	20	3.5										4	7	17	27	59
	25	3.3									2	7	10	24	45	92
	30	3.3									6	7	17	23	59	116
	40	3.2								5	9	17	19	45	79	178
	60	2.7					4	10	10	10	12	22	36	64	126	297
	90	2.2		8	10	10	10	10	10	28	28	44	68	98	186	513
	120															
	180															
	240															
260	5	4.0												1	2	7
	10	3.8											2	4	9	19
	15	3.7										2	4	10	22	42
	20	3.5									1	4	7	20	31	67
	25	3.5									3	8	11	23	50	99
	30	3.3								2	6	8	19	26	61	125
	40	3.2							1	6	11	16	19	49	84	190
270	5	4.2												1	3	9
	10	4.0											2	5	11	22
	15	3.8										3	4	11	24	46
	20	3.7									2	3	9	21	35	74
	25	3.5								2	3	8	13	23	53	106
	30	3.5								3	6	12	22	27	64	138
	40	3.3							5	6	11	17	22	51	88	204
280	5	4.3												2	2	9
	10	4.0										1	2	5	13	25
	15	3.8									1	3	4	11	26	49
	20	3.8									3	4	8	23	39	81
	25	3.7								2	5	7	16	23	56	113
	30	3.5							1	3	7	13	22	30	70	150
	40	3.3						1	6	6	13	17	27	51	93	218
290	5	4.5												2	3	10
	10	4.2										1	3	5	16	30
	15	4.0									1	3	6	12	26	52
	20	4.0									3	7	9	23	43	89
	25	3.8								3	5	8	17	23	60	120
	30	3.7							1	5	6	16	22	36	72	162
	40	3.5						3	5	7	15	16	32	51	95	264
300	5	4.7												3	3	11
	10	4.3										1	3	6	17	32
	15	4.2									2	3	6	15	26	56
	20	4.0								2	3	7	10	23	47	104
	25	3.8							1	3	6	8	19	26	61	128
	30	3.8							2	5	7	17	22	39	75	171
	40	3.7						4	6	9	15	17	34	51	90	234
	60	3.0		4	10	10	10	10	10	14	28	32	50	90	187	458
	90															
	120															
	180															

(Rev. 1958)

Table 1–9.—U. S. Navy standard air decompression table for exceptional exposures.

dive or dives, add the actual bottom time of the previous dives to the actual bottom time of the repetitive dive.

(23) The U. S. Navy Standard Air Decompression Table for Exceptional Exposures (table 1–9) includes only schedules of decompression for exceptional or emergency cases. Schedules are provided for "complete saturation" exposures up to 140 feet, and for extreme exposures up to 300 feet. Great demands are imposed upon the diver's endurance by emergencies which might necessitate use of the table. Therefore complete assurance of success of the schedules is impossible. They have, however, been tested to every practicable limit and found reasonably safe.

(24) Repetitive group designations are not given on the Table for Exceptional Exposures. Never follow a dive covered by that table with a repetitive dive. Make every effort to limit the equivalent single dive schedule of repetitive dives to the Standard Air Decompression Table. The diving officer must be the one to weigh the need for any dive in the Table for Exceptional Exposures against the increased danger and demands on the diver's physical endurance.

(25) Figure 1–32 is a suggested (U. S. Navy) worksheet for the selection of decompression schedules in repetitive diving. A systematic approach of this kind must *always* be used in applying the repetitive diving tables.

(26) In the example using figure 1–32 the diver has made a dive to 105 feet with a bottom time of 24 minutes and decompresses properly according to the Standard Air Decompression Table. After being on the surface for 2 hours, he is required to make a second dive, this time to 145 feet. It is anticipated that 15 minutes' bottom time will be required to complete his work. The problem is to determine the proper decompression for this second or *repetitive dive*. Use the time and depth of his first or *previous dive* in worksheet part I. Table 1–5 indicates that he is in repetitive group "H" (according to the 110/25

schedule). During the surface interval of 2 hours he loses sufficient nitrogen to change from group "H" to group "E" according to the Surface Interval Credit Table (table 1–7). His residual nitrogen time may now be determined using the depth of his second or repetitive dive and the *new* group from the end of the surface interval by referring to the Repetitive Dive Timetable (table 1–8). This indicates that the diver's residual nitrogen time is 12 minutes. The 15 minutes actual bottom time of the repetitive dive is added to the residual nitrogen time to obtain the *equivalent single dive time,* which is 27 minutes. This is used, as indicated in worksheet part V, to select the decompression schedule for the repetitive dive; in this case from table 1–5, the 150/30 schedule.

MORE THAN ONE REPETITIVE DIVE

(27) When one repetitive dive is to be followed by another, the procedure for selecting the proper decompression schedule for the first repetitive dive is *repeated*. The time and depth of the equivalent single dive of the *first* repetitive dive calculation becomes the time and depth of the "previous dive" of the *second* repetitive dive calculation.

SURFACE DECOMPRESSION (RECOMPRESSION)

(1) In surface decompression procedures, stage decompression in the water is reduced to a minimum or eliminated and the major part of decompression is accomplished in a recompression chamber on the surface. Oxygen is the standard breathing medium during the decompression period on the surface. Air or gas mixtures are alternate breathing mediums. There are separate decompression tables and procedures which apply specifically to the breathing medium used.

(2) At present in the U. S. Navy, surface decompression procedures expose the diver to atmospheric pressure for a *brief surface interval* between leaving the water and attaining the scheduled decompression stop depth in the

REPETITIVE DIVE WORKSHEET

I. PREVIOUS DIVE:

24 minutes } see table 1-5 or 1-6 for } } Group *H*
105 feet } repetitive group designation }

II. SURFACE INTERVAL:

2 hours *0* minutes on surface } see table 1-7 } Group *E*
Group *H* (from I.) } for new group }

III. RESIDUAL NITROGEN TIME:

145 feet (depth of repetitive dive) } see table } *12* minutes
Group *E* (from II.) } 1-8 }

IV. EQUIVALENT SINGLE DIVE TIME:

12 minutes (residual nitrogen time from III.)

(add) *15* minutes (actual bottom time of repetitive dive)

(sum) *27* minutes

V. DECOMPRESSION FOR REPETITIVE DIVE:

27 minutes (equivalent single dive } see table }
time from IV.) } }
145 feet (depth of repetitive dive) } 1-5 or 1-6 }

☐ No decompression required

or

Decompression stops: *20* feet *8* minutes
10 feet *24* minutes
_____ feet _____ minutes
_____ feet _____ minutes

Figure 1–32.—Repetitive dive worksheet (filled in).

recompression chamber. The interval *must* be as short as possible.

(3) The principal advantages of surface decompression are the comfort and security of the diver in situations of extremely cold or rough sea, physical exhaustion, and the like. In certain dives, surface decompression with pure oxygen has the additional advantage of saving an appreciable amount of the total decompression time required for straight air decompression.

(4) Surface decompression schedules may be applied to emergencies where a surface interval *must* come between the dive and the

Table columns (per note): Column 1 Depth (ft); Column 2 Time (min); Column 3 Time (min) at water stops breathing air at 60′ 50′ 40′ 30′; Column 4 Surface interval not to exceed 5 minutes; Column 5 Time (min) at 40′ chamber stop oxygen; Column 6 2 minute ascent from 40 feet in chamber to surface while breathing oxygen; Column 7 Approximate total decompression time (min).

1** DEPTH IN FEET	2** TIME	3** 60′	50′	40′	30′	4**	5** CHAMBER STOP OXYGEN	6**	7** TOTAL DECOMP. TIME
70	52	0	0	0	0		0		3
	90	0	0	0	0		15		24
	*120	0	0	0	0		23		32
	150	0	0	0	0		31		40
	180	0	0	0	0		39		48
80	40	0	0	0	0		0		3
	70	0	0	0	0		14		23
	85	0	0	0	0		20		29
	100	0	0	0	0		26		35
	*115	0	0	0	0		31		40
	130	0	0	0	0		37		46
	150	0	0	0	0		44		53
90	32	0	0	0	0		0		4
	60	0	0	0	0		14		24
	70	0	0	0	0		20		30
	80	0	0	0	0		25		35
	*90	0	0	0	0		30		40
	100	0	0	0	0		34		44
	110	0	0	0	0		39		49
	120	0	0	0	0		43		53
	130	0	0	0	0		48		58
100	26	0	0	0	0		0		4
	50	0	0	0	0		14		24
	60	0	0	0	0		20		30
	70	0	0	0	0		26		36
	*80	0	0	0	0		32		42
	90	0	0	0	0		38		48
	100	0	0	0	0		44		54
	110	0	0	0	0		49		59
	120	0	0	0	3		53		66

1** DEPTH IN FEET	2** TIME	3** 60′	50′	40′	30′	4**	5** CHAMBER STOP OXYGEN	6**	7** TOTAL DECOMP. TIME
120	70	0	0	0	4		39		54
	80	0	0	0	4		46		62
	90	0	0	3	7		51		72
	100	0	0	6	15		54		86
130	15	0	0	0	0		0		5
	30	0	0	0	0		12		23
	40	0	0	0	0		21		32
	50	0	0	0	3		29		43
	*60	0	0	0	5		37		53
	70	0	0	0	7		45		63
	80	0	0	6	7		51		76
	90	0	0	10	12		56		90
140	13	0	0	0	0		0		6
	25	0	0	0	0		11		23
	30	0	0	0	0		15		27
	35	0	0	0	0		20		32
	40	0	0	0	2		24		38
	45	0	0	0	4		29		45
	50	0	0	0	6		33		51
	*55	0	0	0	7		38		57
	60	0	0	0	8		43		63
	65	0	0	3	7		48		70
	70	0	2	7	7		51		80
150	11	0	0	0	0		0		6
	25	0	0	0	0		13		25
	30	0	0	0	0		18		30
	35	0	0	0	4		23		39
	40	0	0	3	6		27		49
	45	0	0	5	7		33		58
	*50	0	2	5	8		38		66
	55	2	5	9	4		44		78

1** DEPTH IN FEET	2** TIME	3** 60′	50′	40′	30′	4**	5** CHAMBER STOP OXYGEN	6**	7** TOTAL DECOMP. TIME
110	22	0	0	0	0		0		5
	40	0	0	0	0		12		23
	50	0	0	0	0		19		30
	60	0	0	0	0		26		37
	*70	0	0	0	0		33		44
	80	0	0	0	1		40		52
	90	0	0	0	2		46		59
	100	0	0	0	5		51		67
	110	0	0	0	12		54		77
120	18	0	0	0	0		0		5
	30	0	0	0	0		9		20
	40	0	0	0	0		16		27
	50	0	0	0	0		24		35
	*60	0	0	0	2		32		45

1** DEPTH IN FEET	2** TIME	3** 60′	50′	40′	30′	4**	5** CHAMBER STOP OXYGEN	6**	7** TOTAL DECOMP. TIME
160	9	0	0	0	0		0		7
	20	0	0	0	0		11		24
	25	0	0	0	0		16		29
	30	0	0	0	2		21		35
	35	0	0	4	6		26		49
	40	0	3	5	8		32		62
	*45	3	4	8	6		38		73
170	7	0	0	0	0		0		7
	20	0	0	0	0		13		26
	25	0	0	0	0		19		32
	30	0	0	3	5		23		44
	35	0	4	4	7		29		58
	*40	4	4	8	6		36		73

*These are the optimum exposure times for each depth which represent the best balance between length of work period, safety and amount of useful work for the average diver. Exposure beyond these times is permitted only under special conditions.

**Notes on columns.

Column 1. Depth—In feet, gage.

Column 2. Time—Interval from leaving the surface to leading the bottom.

Column 3. Water stops—Time spent at tabulated stops using air. If no water stops are required use a 25 foot per minute rate of ascent to the surface. When water stops are required use a 25 foot per minute rate of ascent to first stop. Take an additional minute between stops. Use one minute for the ascent from 30 feet to the surface.

Column 4. Surface interval—The surface interval shall not exceed 5 minutes and is composed of the following elements:

(a) Time of ascent from the 30 foot water stop, or from 30 feet if no water stops are necessary, to the surface (1 minute).

(b) Time on surface for landing the diver on deck and undressing (not to exceed 3½ minutes).

(c) Time of descent in the recompression chamber from the surface to 40 feet (about ½ minute).

Column 5. During the period while breathing oxygen the chamber shall be ventilated.

Column 6. Surfacing—Oxygen breathing during this 2-minute period shall follow the period of oxygen breathing tabulated in Column 5 without interruption.

Column 7. Total decompression time—This includes

(a) Time of ascent from bottom to first stop, or to 30 feet if no water stop is required, at 25 feet per minute.

(b) Sum of tabulated water stops, column 2.

(c) One minute between water stops.

(d) Surface interval.

(e) Time at 40 feet in recompression chamber, column 4.

(f) Time of ascent, an additional 2 minutes, from 40 feet in the recompression chamber to the surface, column 5.

The Approximate Total Decompression Time may be shortened only by decreasing the time required to undress the diver on deck.

Table 1–17.—Surface decompression table using oxygen.

major part of the decompression. Such cases may be emergencies forcing unscheduled surfacing or in scuba diving, when the diver *must* surface to obtain a new air supply. Although it is possible when air is the breathing medium for the decompression period following the surface interval to be in the water, *recompression in a chamber if available is always to be preferred.*

(5) If a recompression chamber is available and is equipped with proper oxygen-breathing equipment, the procedure outlined in Surface Decompression Table Using Oxygen (table 1–17) may be used in a routine manner. Follow the instructions accurately and take all precautions to insure that only pure oxygen is breathed. Maintain breathing equipment in perfect working condition to insure successful results from this table.

(6) In the event of oxygen toxicity symptoms, or failure of the oxygen supply, give decompression in accordance with table 1–18, disregarding time spent on oxygen.

(7) Table 1–17 has not been recomputed in accordance with the concepts established in the calculation of the Standard Air Decompression Table. There are some discrepancies in limits of allowable exposures. However, this table is considered to be safe in its present form. Note that ascent at the rate of 25 feet per minute is required for the initial ascent when using this table.

AIR FOLLOWING AN AIR DIVE

(8) The Surface Decompression Table Using Air (table 1–18) may be used in any situation requiring surface decompression when breathing oxygen in a chamber is impossible. Since there is no saving of time over ordinary decompression methods, the comfort and security of the diver are the only advantages for the use of this surface decompression method.

(9) In self-contained diving it may be impossible for the diver to carry sufficient air supply for the duration of the entire dive and standard decompression. When this is the case,

the diver may (according to either table 1–17 or 1–18) surface, and receive the major part of his decompression in a recompression chamber. If no chamber is available, he may (according to table 1–18) take the "water stops" in the water, surface, obtain new air supply, and return in the water to the scheduled stop depths. However, providing surface-supplied air or extra air cylinders for use at the decompression stop depth, with decompression according to standard tables, is a safer and more reasonable procedure.

(10) Table 1–18 requires repetition of one stop and increases the total decompression time required by the same schedule in the Standard Air Decompression Table by that amount. At the moment, there is no procedure outlined for surface decompression following a dive on the Standard Air Decompression Table for Exceptional Exposures.

(11) Ascend from the last water stop to the surface at the rate of 60 feet per minute. Maintain the time on the surface to the absolute minimum. Do not exceed the 3½ minute limit. Descend to the first chamber stop at the normal rate.

OMITTED DECOMPRESSION IN EMERGENCIES

(1) Certain emergencies may interrupt or prevent specified decompression. Complete loss of communication without a standby diver, exhausted air supply, bodily injury, and the like are among such emergencies. If there are symptoms of decompression sickness or air embolism, immediate treatment by recompression is essential. Even without evidence of any ill effects, omitted decompression must be made up in some manner to avert later difficulty.

USE OF SURFACE DECOMPRESSION TABLES

(2) It may *appear* that surface decompression schedules offer an immediate solution to this problem since they provide for a surface interval. Such schedules should *only* be used,

TIME ON SURFACE NOT TO EXCEED 3.5 MINUTES

DEPTH (ft.)	BOT-TOM TIME (Min.)	TIME TO FIRST STOP	TIME AT WATER STOPS			CHAMBER STOPS (AIR)			TOTAL ASCENT TIME
			30	20	10	30	20	10	
40	230	0.5			3			7	10.5
	250	0.5			3			11	14.5
	270	0.5			3			15	18.5
	300	0.5			3			19	22.5
50	120	0.7			3			5	8.7
	140	0.7			3			10	13.7
	160	0.7			3			21	24.7
	180	0.7			3			29	32.7
	200	0.7			3			35	38.7
	220	0.7			3			40	43.7
	240	0.7			3			47	50.7
60	80	0.8			3			7	10.8
	100	0.8			3			14	17.8
	120	0.8			3			26	29.8
	140	0.8			3			39	42.8
	160	0.8			3			48	51.8
	180	0.8			3			56	59.8
	200	0.7		3			3	69	75.7
70	60	1.0			3			8	12.0
	70	1.0			3			14	18.0
	80	1.0			3			18	22.0
	90	1.0			3			23	27.0
	100	1.0			3			33	37.0
	110	0.8		3			3	41	47.8
	120	0.8		3			4	47	54.8
	130	0.8		3			6	52	61.8
	140	0.8		3			8	56	67.8
	150	0.8		3			9	61	73.8
	160	0.8		3			13	72	88.8
	170	0.8		3			19	79	101.8
80	50	1.2			3			10	14.2
	60	1.2			3			17	21.2
	70	1.2			3			23	27.2
	80	1.0		3			3	31	38.0
	90	1.0		3			7	39	50.0
	100	1.0		3			11	46	61.0
	110	1.0		3			13	53	70.0
	120	1.0		3			17	56	77.0
	130	1.0		3			19	63	86.0
	140	1.0		26			26	69	122.0
	150	1.0		32			32	77	142.0
90	40	1.3			3			7	11.3
	50	1.3			3			18	22.3
	60	1.3			3			25	29.3
	70	1.2		3			7	30	41.2
	80	1.2		13			13	40	67.2
	90	1.2		18			18	48	85.2
	100	1.2		21			21	54	97.2
	110	1.2		24			24	61	110.2
	120	1.2		32			32	68	133.2
	130	1.0	5	36			36	74	152.0
100	40	1.5			3			15	19.5
	50	1.3		3			3	24	31.3
	60	1.3		3			9	28	41.3
	70	1.3		3			17	39	60.3
	80	1.3		23			23	48	95.3
	90	1.2	3	23			23	57	107.2
	100	1.2	7	23			23	66	120.2
	110	1.2	10	34			34	72	151.2
	120	1.2	12	41			41	78	173.2
110	30	1.7			3			7	11.7
	40	1.5		3			3	21	28.5
	50	1.5		3			8	26	38.5
	60	1.5		18			18	36	73.5
	70	1.5	1	23			23	48	96.5
	80	1.3	7	23			23	57	111.3
	90	1.3	12	30			30	64	137.3
	100	1.3	15	37			37	72	162.3

DEPTH (ft.)	BOT-TOM TIME (Min.)	TIME TO FIRST STOP	TIME AT WATER STOPS					CHAMBER STOPS (AIR)			TOTAL ASCENT TIME
			50	40	30	20	10	30	20	10	
120	25	1.8					3			6	10.8
	30	1.8					3			14	18.8
	40	1.7				3			5	25	34.7
	50	1.7				15			15	31	62.7
	60	1.5			2	22			22	45	92.5
	70	1.5			9	23			23	55	111.5
	80	1.5			15	27			27	63	133.5
	90	1.5			19	37			37	74	168.5
	100	1.5			23	45			45	80	194.5
130	25	2.0					3			10	15.0
	30	1.8				3			3	18	25.8
	40	1.8				10			10	25	46.8
	50	1.7			3	21			21	37	83.7
	60	1.7			9	23			23	52	108.7
	70	1.7			16	24			24	61	126.7
	80	1.5		3	19	35			35	72	165.5
	90	1.5		8	19	45			45	80	198.5
140	20	2.2					3			6	11.2
	25	2.0				3			3	14	22.0
	30	2.0				5			5	21	33.0
	40	1.8			2	16			16	26	61.8
	50	1.8			6	24			24	44	99.8
	60	1.8			16	23			23	56	119.8
	70	1.7		4	19	32			32	68	156.7
	80	1.7		10	23	41			41	79	195.7
150	20	2.2				3			3	7	15.2
	25	2.2				4			4	17	27.2
	30	2.2				8			8	24	42.2
	40	2.0			5	19			19	33	78.0
	50	2.0			12	23			23	51	111.0
	60	1.8		3	19	26			26	62	137.8
	70	1.8		11	19	39			39	75	184.8
	80	1.7	1	17	19	50			50	84	222.7
160	20	2.3				3			3	11	19.3
	25	2.3				7			7	20	36.3
	30	2.2			2	11			11	25	51.2
	40	2.2			7	23			23	39	94.2
	50	2.0		2	16	23			23	55	121.0
	60	2.0		9	19	33			33	69	165.0
	70	1.8	1	17	22	44			44	80	209.8
170	15	2.5				3			3	5	13.5
	20	2.5				4			4	15	25.5
	25	2.3			2	7			7	23	41.3
	30	2.3			4	13			13	26	58.3
	40	2.2		1	10	23			23	45	104.2
	50	2.2		5	18	23			23	61	132.2
	60	2.0	2	15	22	37			37	74	187.0
	70	2.0	8	17	19	51			51	86	234.0
180	15	2.7				3			3	6	14.7
	20	2.5			1	5			5	17	30.5
	25	2.5			3	10			10	24	49.5
	30	2.5			6	17			17	27	69.5
	40	2.3		3	14	23			23	50	115.3
	50	2.2	2	9	19	30			30	65	155.2
	60	2.2	5	16	19	44			44	81	211.2
190	15	2.8				4			4	7	17.8
	20	2.7			2	6			6	20	36.7
	25	2.7			5	11			11	25	54.7
	30	2.5		1	8	19			19	32	81.5
	40	2.5		8	14	23			23	55	125.5
	50	2.3	4	13	22	33			33	72	179.3
	60	2.3	10	17	19	50			50	84	232.3

Table 1–18.—Surface decompression table using air.

however, *if the emergency surface interval occurs at such a time that "water stops" are not required or have already been completed* according to whichever surface decompression table is considered most appropriate.

SURFACE DECOMPRESSION TABLES NOT APPLICABLE

(3) When the conditions in paragraph (2) are *not* fulfilled, the diver's decompression has been compromised. Special care should be taken to detect signs of decompression sickness regardless of what action is initiated. The diver must be returned to pressure as soon as possible. Use of a recompression chamber, if available, is always preferable to water decompression.

WHEN A RECOMPRESSION CHAMBER IS AVAILABLE

(4) Even if the diver shows no ill effects from his omitted decompression, he needs immediate recompression. Take him to 100 feet in the chamber and keep him at that depth for 30 minutes. If he is still all right after that time, bring him out according to TREATMENT TABLE 1 or 1-A. (See table 1–21.) Consider decompression sickness developing during or after this as a recurrence. (See table 1–22.)

IN WATER

WHEN NO CHAMBER IS AVAILABLE

(5) Recompress the diver in the water, following the procedure in paragraph (4) as nearly as possible. Keep the diver at rest, provide a standby diver, and maintain good communication and depth control.

(6) When the course of action outlined in paragraph (5) is impossible, use the following procedure which is based on the Standard Air Decompression Table:

(*a*) Repeat any stops deeper than 40 feet.
(*b*) At 40 feet, remain for ¼ of the 10-foot stop time.
(*c*) At 30 feet, remain for ⅓ of the 10-foot stop time.
(*d*) At 20 feet, remain for ½ of the 10-foot stop time.
(*e*) At 10 feet, remain for 1½ times the scheduled 10-foot stop time.

Table 1–22

NOTES ON RECOMPRESSION

Explanation: All references to TABLES *indicate parts of table 1–21 "Treatment of Decompression Sickness and Air Embolism."*

1. *General Considerations*

   a. Follow TREATMENT TABLES (table 1–21) accurately.
   b. Permit no shortening or other alteration of tables except on advice of trained *diving medical officer* or in extreme emergency.

2. *Rate of Descent in Chamber*

   a. Normal rate is 25 feet per minute.
   b. Serious symptoms: rapid descent is desirable.
   c. If pain increases on descent: stop, resume at a rate tolerated by patient.

3. *Treatment Depth*

   a. Go to full depth indicated by table required.
   b. Do not go beyond 165 feet except on decision of medical officer.

4. *Examination of Patient*

   a. If no serious symptoms are evident and pain is not severe, examine thoroughly before treatment.
   b. If any serious symptom is noted, do not delay descent for examination or for determining depth of relief.
   c. In "pain only" cases where relief is reported before reaching 66 feet, make sure it is complete before deciding on TABLE 1.

STOPS	BENDS—PAIN ONLY		SERIOUS SYMPTOMS	
Rate of descent —25 ft. per min. Rate of ascent— 1 minute between stops.	Pain relieved at depths less than 66 ft. Use table 1—A if O₂ is not available.	Pain relieved at depths greater than 66 ft. Use table 2—A if O₂ is not available. If pain does not improve within 30 min. at 165 ft. the case is probably not bends. Decompress on table 2 or 2—A.	Serious symptoms include any one of the following: 1. Unconsciousness. 2. Convulsions. 3. Weakness or inability to use arms or legs. 4. Air embolism. 5. Any visual disturbances. 6. Dizziness. 7. Loss of speech or hearing. 8. Severe shortness of breath or chokes. 9. Bends occurring while still under pressure.	
			Symptoms relieved within 30 minutes at 165 ft. Use table 3	Symptoms not relieved within 30 minutes at 165 ft. Use table 4

POUNDS	FEET	TABLE 1	TABLE 1-A	TABLE 2	TABLE 2-A	TABLE 3	TABLE 4
73.4	165	....	....	30 (air)	30 (air)	30 (air)	30 to 120 (air)
62.3	140	....	....	12 (air)	12 (air)	12 (air)	30 (air)
53.4	120	....	....	12 (air)	12 (air)	12 (air)	30 (air)
44.5	100	30 (air)	30 (air)	12 (air)	12 (air)	12 (air)	30 (air)
35.6	80	12 (air)	12 (air)	12 (air)	12 (air)	12 (air)	30 (air)
26.7	60	30 (O₂)	30 (air)	30 (O₂)	30 (air)	30 (O₂) or (air)	6 hrs. (air)
22.3	50	30 (O₂)	30 (air)	30 (O₂)	30 (air)	30 (O₂) or (air)	6 hrs. (air)
17.8	40	30 (O₂)	30 (air)	30 (O₂)	30 (air)	30 (O₂) or (air)	6 hrs. (air)
13.4	30	5 (O₂)	60 (air)	60 (O₂)	2 hrs. (air)	12 hrs. (air)	First 11 hrs. (air) Then 1 hr. (O₂) or (air)
8.9	20	5 (O₂)	60 (air)	5 (O₂)	2 hrs. (air)	2 hrs. (air)	First 1 hr. (air) Then 1 hr. (O₂) or (air)
4.5	10	5 (O₂)	2 hrs. (air)	5 (O₂)	4 hrs. (air)	2 hrs. (air)	First 1 hr. (air) Then 1 hr. (O₂) or (air)
Surface			1 min. (air)		1 min. (air)	1 min. (air)	1 min. (O₂)

Time at all stops in minutes unless otherwise indicated.

Table 1–21.—Treatment of Decompression Sickness and Air Embolism.

d. On reaching maximum depth of treatment, examine as completely as possible to detect
   1) Incomplete relief
   2) Any symptoms overlooked
   NOTE.—At the very least, have patient stand and walk length of chamber.
e. Recheck before leaving bottom.
f. Ask patient how he feels before and after coming to each stop and periodically during long stops.
g. Do not let patient sleep through changes of depth or for more than an hour at a time at any stop. (Symptoms can develop or recur during sleep.)
h. Recheck patient before leaving last stop.

5. *Patient Getting Worse*

   a. Never continue bringing a patient up if his condition is worsening.
   b. Treat as a *recurrence during treatment* (see 6).
   c. Consider use of helium-oxygen as breathing medium for patient (see 8).

6. *Recurrence of Symptoms*

   a. *During* treatment:
      1) Take patient to depth of relief (but never to less than 30 feet; and not deeper than 165 feet except on decision of medical officer).
      (If recurrence involves serious symptom not previously present, take patient to 165 feet.)
      2) Complete the treatment according to TABLE 4.
   b. *Following* treatment:
      1) Recompress to depth giving relief.
      2) If depth of relief is less than 30 feet,
         a) Take to 30 feet.
         b) Decompress from 30-foot stop according to TABLE 3.
      3) If relief occurs deeper than 30 feet,
         a) Keep patient at depth of relief for 30 minutes.
         b) Complete remaining stops of TABLE 3.
         NOTE.—If original treatment was on TABLE 3, use TABLE 4.
      4) Examine carefully to be sure no serious symptom is present. If the original treatment was on TABLE 1 or TABLE 2, appearance of a serious symptom requires full treatment on TABLE 3 or TABLE 4.

ALWAYS KEEP DIVER CLOSE TO CHAMBER FOR AT LEAST 6 HOURS AFTER TREATMENT. (Keep him for 24 hours unless very prompt return can be assured.)

7. *Use of Oxygen*

   a. Use oxygen wherever permitted by tables unless
      1) Patient has not had oxygen tolerance test, or
      2) Is known to tolerate oxygen poorly.
   b. Be sure mask fits snugly.
   c. Take all precautions against fire.
   d. Tend carefully, being alert for symptoms of oxygen poisoning such as
      1) Twitching
      2) Dizziness
      3) Nausea
      4) Blurring of vision
   e. Know what to do in event of convulsion. Have mouth-bit available.
   f. If symptoms appear, remove mask at once.
   g. If oxygen breathing must be interrupted—
      1) On TABLE 1, proceed on TABLE 1–A.
      2) On TABLE 2, proceed on TABLE 2–A.
      3) On TABLE 3, continue on TABLE 3 using air.
   h. At medical officer's discretion, oxygen breathing may be resumed at 40-foot stop. If this is done, complete treatment as follows:
      1) Resuming from TABLE 1–A: breathe oxygen:
         at 40 feet for 30 minutes
         at 30 feet for 1 hour
      2) Resuming from TABLE 2–A: breathe oxygen:
         at 40 feet for 30 minutes
         at 30 feet for 2 hours
      3) In both cases, then surface in 5 minutes still breathing oxygen
      4) Resuming from TABLE 3: breathe oxygen:
         at 40 feet for 30 minutes
         at 30 feet for first hour
         (then finish treatment with air)

MOST FREQUENT ERRORS RELATED TO TREATMENT

1. Diver's failure to report symptoms early.
2. Failure to treat doubtful cases.
3. Failure to treat promptly.
4. Failure to recognize serious symptoms.
5. Failure to treat adequately.
6. Failure to keep patient near chamber after treatment.

8. *Use of Helium-Oxygen*

   a. Helium-oxygen mixtures (ratio about 80:20) can be used *instead of air* (not in place of oxygen) in all types of treatment and at any depth.

   b. Use of helium-oxygen is especially desirable in any patient who

   1) Has serious symptoms that fail to clear within a short time at 165 feet.

   2) Has recurrence or otherwise becomes worse at any stage of treatment.

   3) Has any difficulty in breathing.

9. *Tenders*

   a. A qualified tender must be in chamber

   1) If patient has had any serious symptom.

   2) Whenever patient is breathing oxygen.

   3) When patient needs unusual observation or care for any reason.

   b. Tender must be alert for any change in patient, especially during oxygen breathing. (See 7, d–f.)

   c. *Tender must breathe oxygen* if he has been with patient throughout TABLE 1 or TABLE 2

   TABLE 1: Breathe oxygen—
      at 40 feet for 30 minutes

   TABLE 2: Breathe oxygen—
      at 30 feet for 1 hour

   d. Tender in chamber only through oxygen breathing part of TABLE 1 or 2 gains safety-factor by breathing oxygen for 30 minutes of last stop, but this is not essential. Tender may breathe oxygen during use of TABLE 3 or 4 at 40 feet or less.

   e. Anyone entering chamber and leaving before completion of treatment must be decompressed according to standard diving tables.

   f. Personnel outside must specify and control decompression of anyone leaving chamber and must review all decisions concerning treatment or decompression made by personnel (including medical officer) inside chamber.

10. *Ventilation of Chamber*

   Rule 1. Volume of air required (volume as measured at chamber pressure—applies at any depth):

   a. Basic requirement:

   1) Allow 2 cubic feet per minute per man.

   2) *Add* 2 cubic feet per minute for each man *not at rest* (as tender actively taking care of patient).

   b. When using oxygen:
   Allow 4 cubic feet of *air per man breathing oxygen* if this yields larger figure than basic requirements. (Do not add to basic requirement.)

   Rule 2. Maximum interval between ventilations:

   a. Not using oxygen:
   Interval (min.)

   $$\frac{\text{Chamber (or lock) volume (cu. ft.)}}{\text{Basic vent. req. (cu. ft./min.) (from rule 1)}}$$

   b. Using oxygen:
   Interval (min.)

   $$\frac{\text{Chamber (or lock) vol. (cu. ft.)}}{\text{No. of men br. O}_2 \times 10}$$

   a. Timing of ventilation:

   1) Use any convenient interval shorter than maximum from rule 2.

   2) (Continuous steady-rate ventilation is also satisfactory.)

   b. Volume used at each ventilation:

   1) Multiply volume requirement (cu. ft./min.) from rule 1 by number of minutes since start of last ventilation.

   c. Use predetermined exhaust valve settings to obtain required volume of ventilation.

11. *First Aid*

   a. First aid measures may be required in addition to recompression. Do not neglect them.

12. *Recompression in the Water*

   a. Recompression without a chamber is difficult and hazardous. Except in grave emergency, seek nearest chamber even if at considerable distance.

   b. If water recompression must be used and diver is conscious and able to care for himself:

   1) Use deep sea diving rig if available.

   2) Follow treatment tables as closely as possible.

   3) Maintain constant communication.

   4) Have standby diver ready.

   c. If diver is unconscious or incapacitated, send another diver with him to control his valves and otherwise assist him.

   d. If lightweight diving outfit or scuba must be used, keep at least one diver with patient at all times. Plan carefully for shifting rigs or cylinders. Have ample number of tenders topside and at intermediate depths.

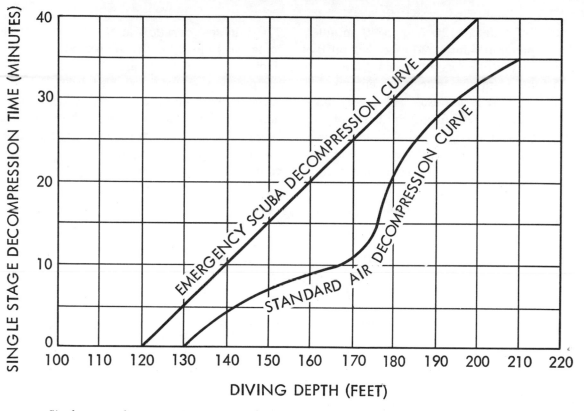

Single-stage decompression curves showing standard decompression and emergency decompression for fifteen minutes of bottom time. Standard curve concurs exactly with U. S. Navy Decompression Tables, whereas the emergency curve is a straight-line approximation (well on the safe side) for the sake of convenience and rapidity.

e. If depth is inadequate for full treatment according to tables:

1) Take patient to maximum available depth.

2) Keep him there 30 minutes.

3) Bring him up according to TABLE 3 if he can tolerate exposure. (If patient has been taken beyond 100 feet, do not use stops shorter than those of TABLE 2–A.)

(End of Table 1–22.)

ONE-STOP DECOMPRESSION FOR EMERGENCY DIVES

If an auxiliary air supply is available for decompression, you may terminate your dive when you reach the low-air-supply warning, ascend at the standard sixty-foot-per-minute rate to your first decompression stage, and take decompression according to the Standard Compressed Air Decompression Tables on pages 112 and 117 for whatever your depth and time happen to be. In many cases, you may require stops deeper than ten feet, but suppose you found it desirable to control your deep dive so that you could complete your decompression time using your original aqualung in only a single decompression stop?

A plot of decompression time against depth for fifteen-minute dives between 130 and 210 feet with the old (pre-1958) Standard Air Decompression Tables gives the curve shown here. The straight line drawn from zero decompression time at 120 feet to 40 minutes of decompression time at 200 feet lies on the safe side of the old decompression curve (using 25-foot-per-minute rate of ascent instead of 60), and there is a considerable safety margin. The straight line forms the basis of the emergency deep-diving rules of thumb given below, which are expressed concisely in the graph. This table applies to any double standard compressed-air-tank block giving at least 120 minutes' duration at the surface for the same work load as that expected at bottom depth. It is meant for use when auxiliary decompression is not available and all decompression must be taken on the original aqualung air tank. The decreasing bottom times beyond 140 feet reflect the conservation of air supply necessary to complete the required decompression at the single 10-foot stop.

Chapter 9

DIAGNOSIS AND TREATMENT OF DIVING ACCIDENTS

Since I am no physician, I have relied almost entirely upon the medical personnel of the U. S. Navy Experimental Diving Unit, the Medical Research Laboratory at the Submarine Escape Training School, the *U. S. Navy Diving Manual,* and the U. S. Navy *Manual for Submarine Medicine Practice,* which I consider the ultimate authorities on diving first aid. The following pages contain a list, gathered from these sources, of all diving accidents and diseases in alphabetical order, together with their causes, signs (indications visible to an observer), symptoms (indications experienced by the victim), and treatment. This information has been read, corrected, and updated by Dr. Charles Aquadro, former naval commander with the U. S. Navy Medical Laboratory, New London, Connecticut, one of the world's leading authorities on submarine medicine and now chief medical adviser to Captain Jacques-Yves Cousteau and the Oceanographic Museum of Monaco.

AIR EMBOLISM AND RELATED ACCIDENTS

Air embolism and its related conditions, subcutaneous emphysema, mediastinal emphysema, and pneumothorax, are caused by overexpansion of the lungs by excessive air pressure during a diving ascent, with the resultant tearing of lung tissue and leakage of air. The most common cause of these conditions is voluntary breath-holding during ascent from depths of seven feet or more. (See page 43.)

Air embolism refers to the leakage of air bubbles directly from the lungs into the blood stream. It is the most serious of the embolic diseases, because air bubbles are likely to lodge in the brain and cause rapid and permanent damage there.

Subcutaneous emphysema refers to escaped lung air that has lodged in tissue just beneath the skin, causing a swelling. This usually occurs around the neck and collarbone areas.

Mediastinal emphysema refers to the presence of pockets of air that have escaped from the lungs into the area surrounding the heart, great vessels, trachea, larynx, etc.

Though not very serious in themselves, the presence of either kind of emphysema may indicate the presence of air embolism.

Pneumothorax refers to the presence of air pockets between the lungs and the walls of the chest cavity, which can cause collapse of a lung and extreme difficulty in breathing.

Air embolism. Signs and symptoms are likely to occur *within seconds* of surfacing and to be dramatic in impact. The effects may begin long before the surface is reached, but sometimes a diver will not reveal any signs and symptoms before he loses consciousness.

SYMPTOMS:

weakness

dizziness

paralysis or weakness of limbs

visual disturbance such as blurring

unconsciousness

(all of which indicate brain involvement)

possibly chest pain

SIGNS:

bloody, frothy sputum

staggering

confusion or difficulty in seeing (bumping into objects or moving in wrong direction)

paralysis or weakness of limbs

collapse

unconsciousness

convulsions

cessation of breathing

(*Note:* Onset may be so rapid that only the more serious signs are visible.)

Mediastinal Emphysema. Signs and symptoms are likely to be manifest on surfacing, and result from direct pressure on the heart and large blood vessels.

SYMPTOMS:

pain under breast bone

shortness of breath

faintness

SIGNS:

blueness or cyanosis of skin, lips, or fingernails

difficulty in breathing

shock

possibly voice changes

Subcutaneous emphysema. There are usually no symptoms connected with this malady except in very extreme cases.

POSSIBLE SYMPTOMS:

feeling of fullness in neck area

change in sound of voice

SIGNS:

swelling and inflammation around neck

crackling sensation when skin is moved slightly

change in sound of voice

difficulty in breathing and swallowing

Pneumothorax. Signs and symptoms are likely to be manifest on surfacing.

SYMPTOMS:

sharp pain in chest, usually made worse by deep breathing

shortness of breath

SIGNS:

blueness or cyanosis of skin, lips, or fingernails

evidence of pain

favoring affected side of chest

rapid, shallow breathing

TREATMENT:

Air embolism. Recompress the victim at once to reduce the size of the air bubble and restore proper circulation. The slightest delay may be fatal.

If a recompression chamber is immediately available, send him down to 165 feet as quickly as possible without observing standard rate of descent. If the victim completely recovers within thirty minutes, follow Table 3 in the decompression-sickness and air embolism treatment table on page 124. If he does not recover within thirty minutes, follow Table 4 on the same page.

If no recompression chamber is immediately available, the chances are against you. You may be able to save the victim, however, if you do not lose a second, after the first sign or symptom of air embolism, in getting him to a pressure chamber while he is still able to act rationally. There, complete relief is obtainable.

When the victim is under pressure, follow Table 3 or 4 in the decompression-treatment table on page 124 if possible. Make sure that he has a tender diver by his side at all times. Send immediately for medical help and more air if required, or radio the U. S. Coast Guard.

Emphysema. In cases of mediastinal or subcutaneous emphysema that are not complicated by the presence of air embolism, recompression may not be desirable. Seek medical help immediately and administer oxygen when possible.

Pneumothorax. If uncomplicated by the presence of air embolism, do not recompress. Seek medical help immediately and administer oxygen when possible. Keep the victim resting.

Note: If breathing should stop during treatment, artificial respiration (page 136) (possibly with recompression) should be given to help all other treatment until breathing returns to normal. In case of air embolism, artificial respiration can be administered while the victim is in or being transported to a recompression chamber. Shock must also be treated where it exists, but it does not take precedence over other treatments.

ANOXIA (OXYGEN DEFICIENCY), ASPHYXIA, AND CARBON DIOXIDE POISONING

For all practical purposes, anoxia, asphyxia, and carbon dioxide (excess) poisoning are closely similar in cause, prevention symptoms, and treatment. All can be caused by the loss or inadequacy of an air supply, but CO_2 poisoning can be caused by a build-up of an excessive partial pressure of CO_2 within an air supply as well. Excess of CO_2 is known to complicate cases of the bends and nitrogen narcosis. For example, breathing from a tank that has been mistakenly filled with a gas other than pure air can cause all three. So can overexertion, excessive breath-holding, shallow-water blackout during snorkel diving, excessive pace or skip-breathing, or obstructed air passages.

All three conditions can be prevented by avoiding the causes: by resting when breathing becomes labored, by not hyperventilating or overtaxing your breath-holding limits, and by seeking fresh air if you can't catch your breath.

SYMPTOMS:

> sometimes no warning, as in sudden blackout
> usually acute air hunger
> panting
> fogging of mask
> feeling of intoxication, mental confusion
> headache, dizziness, weakness, sweating, or nausea
> spots before the eyes

SIGNS:

> cyanosis (blueness of skin, nailbeds, and lips)
> slowing of responses, confusion like drunkenness
> unconsciousness if severe
> possible violent increase in breathing, followed by cessation of breathing
> if unconscious, possible muscular twitching

TREATMENT:

Be moderate in breath-holding and skip-breathing. When you feel air hunger or the need to pant, then stop and rest, breathing regularly and deeply, until breathing returns to normal. When doing heavy work with an aqualung, anticipate the need to pant and start breathing deeply. Surface if you cannot catch your breath. If you are treating a victim, remove any obstructions for air passages (including tongue if the diver is unconscious). Usually the exposure to fresh air quickly remedies all three maladies. If he is unconscious, treat according to table on page 151.

Artificial Respiration (see "Drowning," page 136).

ASPHYXIA (see "Anoxia," page 131).

BARNACLE AND MUSSEL CUTS

Much of our coastline is thickly populated by sharp-edged shellfish, such as barnacles and mussels, which can cause severe cuts and abrasions to divers who are thrown in contact with them by wave action while entering and leaving the water. Such areas should be avoided if possible. Cleanse the cuts with soap and fresh water, apply antiseptic bandage, and treat generally as a physical injury.

BARRACUDA BITE

Barracuda have been known to attack divers. Their bite is similar to a dog's. It should be cleansed thoroughly, disinfected, and treated as a physical injury.

THE BENDS (see "Decompression sickness," (page 133).

BLACKOUT (see "Anoxia, Carbon dioxide poisoning," page 131).

BLEEDING

Bleeding, whether internal or external, indicates the presence of some other malady. External bleeding from cuts, etc., should be stopped immediately by using bandages, pressure points or, if necessary, a tourniquet. Internal bleeding after diving may indicate the presence of air embolism and related maladies.

BODY SQUEEZE (see "Squeeze," page 149).

CAISSON'S DISEASE (see "Decompression sickness," page 133).

CARBON DIOXIDE POISONING (see "Anoxia, Asphyxia," page 131).

CARBON MONOXIDE POISONING

Carbon monoxide poisoning is usually caused by contamination of a diver's air supply by carbon monoxide fumes. The presence of carbon monoxide in breathing air prevents the blood from carrying sufficient amounts of oxygen by saturating the hemoglobin. The result is that the body tissues are starved for oxygen (tissue anoxia).

Carbon monoxide poisoning can be prevented by seeing to it that your air supply is always certified pure. Air sources should be tested periodically for traces of carbon monoxide, and compressors should be maintained in tip-top working order. Be certain that the compressor air intakes are as far removed from engine exhausts as possible and upwind. A long extension tube fitted onto the engine exhaust will facilitate this.

SYMPTOMS:

sometimes none before unconsciousness sets in

headache, nausea, dizziness, weakness, tightness in head

confusion and clumsiness similar to drunkenness or anoxia

SIGNS:

slow response, clumsiness, bad judgment

unconsciousness

breathing stops in severe cases

abnormal redness of lips, fingernails, and skin

blood is extremely red

TREATMENT:

Get victim into fresh air as soon as possible and give him oxygen if available. If unconscious, treat accordingly (page 151). Victim will usually recover rapidly with exposure to fresh air, but may suffer lingering aftereffects, such as headache and nausea.

CARDIAC ARREST (see "Heart failure," page 145).

COMPRESSED-AIR ILLNESS (see "Decompression sickness," page 133).

CONE SHELL POISONING

There are more than four hundred species of cone shells in the sea, and all contain a highly developed venom apparatus, some of which can cause death. If disturbed, the tiny, sluglike animal within can thrust out a cluster of microscopic venom-filled teeth that can easily puncture the skin. Although they are beautiful to look at and are prized collector's items, divers should avoid contact, or at least wear heavy gloves when handling them.

SYMPTOMS:

> sharp stinging or burning sensation
> local shut-off of blood supply
> numbness and abnormal sensations may spread from the sting throughout the entire body, particularly the lips and mouth

SIGNS:

> paralysis may follow in severe cases
> local cyanosis (blueness)
> coma and heart failure in severe cases

TREATMENT:

There is no specific treatment for cone shell stings. Cone shell poisoning should be treated as external fish poisoning (page 143).

CORAL CUTS

Almost all divers in tropical waters encounter coral formations, which can cause severe cuts and abrasions upon contact. Although usually not serious, coral wounds are extremely bothersome, itchy, slow to heal, and inducive to infection. A few corals produce a slow-healing, oozing type of wound by means of stinging cells similar to those of jellyfish, though not so violent. A few corals, such as brown mustard coral, produce a burning sting that soon leaves without aftereffects.

Coral wounds can easily be prevented by wearing gloves, shirts, and other protective clothing when diving amid coral formations.

SYMPTOMS AND SIGNS:

> light pain
> inflammation of local area
> severe itching
> red welt formation
> lingering, oozing wound

TREATMENT:

1. Rinse area with baking soda or weak ammonia solution if available; follow with soap and fresh water.

2. Use cortisone ointment or antihistamine cream on the wound and give antihistamine by mouth to reduce initial pain and reaction.

3. As soon as pain begins to subside, cleanse wound thoroughly with soap and water to remove all foreign matter. Apply an antiseptic and dressing.

4. In severe cases (as when washed against coral head by surf) give patient bed rest and elevate affected limbs. Apply kaolin poultices or dressings wet with magnesium sulfate and glycerine solution.

CRAMPS

Overexertion of untrained muscles, extreme heat or cold, and diving too soon after meals sometimes causes a muscle or group of muscles to contract involuntarily and cause great pain. If cramps occur in the water, the pain can be relieved by firmly pressing the affected muscle and then working it out with gentle massage. Or, if you can return to boat or shore, the application of heat to the affected area will provide quick relief.

DECOMPRESSION SICKNESS

Decompression sickness (also known as the bends, Caisson's disease, compressed-air illness, and diver's disease) is caused by the formation of gas bubbles in the blood stream due to inadequate decompression or desaturation of gases following a dive (see page 48). A man cannot have decompression sickness unless he has been exposed to a sudden decrease in ambient pressure, as in caisson work or diving, and if signs and symptoms appear, but not before twelve to fifteen hours after exposure, the chances are that the signs and symptoms are not those of decompression sickness. Generally speaking, the likelihood of decompression sickness increases in proportion to the depth-time ratio and the amount of work involved in a dive; it increases drastically when a diver does not receive stage decompression in accordance with the U. S. Navy Standard Air Decompression Tables on pages 112 and 117. The fact that decompression (the act of decompressing) was carried out in exact accordance with those tables does not rule out the possibility of decompression sickness, however, for a casualty factor of about five percent is considered normal in decompression dives, even when the decompression tables are followed to the letter.

The proper diagnosis of decompression sickness must depend upon an evaluation of the factors involved in the dive—depth, time, recommended decompression time, and workload—and the signs and symptoms manifest in the diver. Signs and symptoms of decompression sickness are usually apparent shortly after surfacing and almost always before twelve hours have elapsed. A review of U. S. Navy data concerning the onset of signs and symptoms of decompression sickness following a dive reveals:

50% occurred within 30 minutes
85% occurred within 1 hour
95% occurred within 3 hours
 1% occurred after 6 hours

SYMPTOMS of decompression sickness have been found to occur with the following frequency:

local pain	89%
leg	70%
arm	30%
dizziness (the "staggers")	5.3%
paralysis	2.3%
shortness of breath (the chokes)	1.6%
extreme fatigue and pain	1.3%
collapse with unconsciousness	0.5%

SIGNS:
  evidences of local pain
  the staggers—clumsiness and lack of response as if drunk
  paralysis or partial paralysis
  blotchy and mottled rash on skin
  shortness of breath
  collapse with unconsciousness
  visual disturbance; extreme fatigue

A typical case of decompression sickness may begin with localized itching or burning, or a tingling, numb sensation, and sometimes with the feeling that ants are crawling over the victim; the most frequent and dominating symptom is a deep boring pain in the bones or joints which becomes progressively worse. A muscle strain or joint sprain suffered during a dive is sometimes confused with decompression sickness. However, sprains and strains are usually painful to touch and accompanied by swelling and discoloration, whereas, areas affected by the bends are not. The dizziness and ringing in the ears that accompany middle-ear damage, usually caused by squeeze, can also be confused with that experienced in decompression sickness. When in doubt, however, treat the diver as if he had the bends, for failure to treat doubtful cases is the most frequent cause of lasting injury.

The most serious signs and symptoms of decompression sickness are those resulting from bubbles in the brain, spinal cord, or lungs. Paralysis, the "chokes," unconsciousness, loss of speech or hearing, convulsions, or dizziness must be treated accordingly (see treatment on pages 123 and 124).

Examination. One fairly safe way to diagnose the presence of decompression sickness is to run through the following U. S. Navy checklist while examining the victim. If need be, ask the victim to walk or do light exercises to provoke manifestation of any of the more serious symptoms.

How does he feel? Any pain? Where and how severe? Changed by motion? Sore to touch or pressure? Bruise marks in the area? Mentally clear? Weakness, numbness, or peculiar sensations anywhere? Can he see and hear clearly? Can he walk, talk, and use his hands normally? Any dizziness?

Does he look and act normal? (Don't just take his word for it if he says he is all right.) Can he walk normally? Any limping or staggering? Is his speech clear and sensible? Is he clumsy or does he seem to be having difficulty with any movement? Can he keep his balance when standing with his eyes closed?

Does he have normal strength? (Check his strength against your own and compare his right side with his left.) Normal hand grip? Able to push and pull strongly with both arms and legs? Able to do deep-knee bends and other exercises?

Are his sensations normal? Can he hear clearly? Can he see clearly both close (reading) and distant objects? Normal vision in all directions? Can he feel pin pricks and light touches with a wisp of cotton all over his body? (Note that some areas are normally less sensitive than others—compare with yourself if in doubt.)

Look at his eyes. Are the pupils of normal size and equal? Do the pupils constrict when you shine a light in his eyes? Can he follow an object around normally with his eyes?

Check his reflexes if you know how. Note that it should not take a great deal of time to examine a man reasonably well.

If the victim is not suffering more than local pain, examine him on the surface, but do not waste time if serious symptoms make decompression sickness obvious. Get him into a recompression chamber or, as a last resort, back under the water and complete your examination there.

TREATMENT:

If there seems to be the slightest possibility that decompression sickness exists, you do not have a second to lose. Recompress the victim according to the U. S. Navy Recompression (Surface Decompression) Treatment Tables on pages 120 and 122. If a recompression chamber is handy, by all means use it, but if it is not, get the victim to proper water depth and call for medical assistance and, if needed, more air immediately. Radio the local U. S. Coast Guard search and rescue squad for an air ambulance if necessary.

DERMATITIS

Frequent and continued exposure to water, especially tropical salt waters and contaminated waters, encourages skin disorders such as fungus infections, eczema, and allergies. While not very serious in themselves, they can incapacitate a man if neglected, and ruin an otherwise perfect diving excursion.

SYMPTOMS:

    red rashes

    welts

    severe itching without obvious cause

    burning sensation when sweating

SIGNS:

    inflammation of affected areas, blotchy
      complexion, welts

    affected skin splitting or peeling

    rashes

    exudation of fluid

TREATMENT:

Dermatitis is best attacked by preventive treatment. Dry thoroughly after each exposure to water. Remove rubber suits, swim suits, wet clothing, supporters, and so forth as soon as possible. Keep such articles clean. Pay particular attention to your toes, ears, armpits, and crotch. Clean and dry them thoroughly and, if affected, sprinkle with medicinal powder. Avoid contamination by scratching, and treat evidence of skin infections with antiseptic or cortisone ointments and bandage. Avoid contaminated waters, and if you are allergic to certain aquatic plants avoid them or wear protective clothing. Do not aggravate infections by continuing to dive before they heal. Seek a cool, dry climate. See a doctor if trouble persists.

DROWNING

Drowning is the cause of over eighty-five percent of all deaths that occur in free diving. It is usually the direct result of some other condition or mishap—usually air embolism—but the result is still the same. Failure of breathing regulator or air supply, loss or flooding of mask or mouthpiece, surface exposure to rough water, overexertion or exhaustion, unconsciousness, electrocution, heart failure, or almost any mishap in water followed by failure of an emergency procedure or by panic can cause the victim to drown.

Adequate training and proper equipment (including flotation gear) and the heeding of all safety precautions are your best assurance against drowning. Your second-best assurance is to ascertain that everyone in your diving party is prepared to aid a diver in distress and is thoroughly schooled in the various methods of administering artificial respiration.

SIGNS:
unconsciousness
cyanosis (blueness)
cessation of breathing
gurgling sounds when stomach is depressed

TREATMENT:

There is only one treatment for drowning or cessation of breathing, and that is immediate application of artificial respiration.

Artificial respiration methods. A mechanical resuscitator is by far the most effective way of applying artificial respiration, but if one is not available there are five ways to administer artificial respiration manually. They are the back-pressure, arm-lift method, the hip-roll, back-pressure method, the bear-hug, arm-lift method, the chest-pressure, arm-lift method, and the mouth-to-mouth method. Of these five, the mouth-to-mouth method is probably the easiest and most immediately available that can be used by free divers, because it can be applied by a buddy diver while the victim is still in the water. If the victim is already out of the water before the operator can get to him, then the back-pressure, arm-lift method or, again, the mouth-to-mouth method is recommended.

The U. S. Navy's recommendations pertaining to methods of emergency artificial respiration are illustrated in this chapter. Every serious diver should familiarize himself with the photo illustrations and practice the procedures until they become second nature.

Administering artificial respiration in the water can be effected by either the standard mouth-to-mouth method or by the snorkel-to-mouth system, which I developed. Where there is no life buoy or float, the snorkel is best. When you reach the surface with the victim (see illustration), do not change position. Inflate all emergency flotation gear if you have not already done so. If the victim's mask is flooded, lift a corner of it up to allow the water to drain and then replace it. Make sure that the victim has not swallowed his tongue by inserting your fingers in his mouth and pulling it forward. If the victim is wearing a snorkel tube, clear it by blowing through the open end, which should be facing you. Insert the mouthpiece into the victim's mouth and hold it shut by cupping your hand under his chin and over his mouth. Then blow into the tube until you feel his chest fully expanded. If the mask rides up and allows air to escape, you must hold it down to maintain an airtight seal. (If this doesn't work, remove his mask and pinch his nostrils shut.) When the victim's lungs are fully inflated, relax your mouth and allow him to exhale automatically. Repeat the process as fast as you can for a full minute and then go into a normal (under the circumstances) breathing rate, blowing all your breath into his lungs and letting him exhale it each time. Do not stop before a rescue boat has arrived with help, and continue resuscitation as he is brought aboard. If need be, you can swim and tow your victim as you give him artificial respiration in this manner.

If you suddenly feel that the victim's chest is not inflating when you blow, it means his air passages have become blocked and you must clear his mouth and tongue once more.

If a life buoy or float is nearby when you surface, it will greatly facilitate both towing and artificial respiration. Your first duty is to tow your victim to the float and slide it or flip it under his chest while you bring his arms down over the outside rim of it, or flip it over his head after releasing the quick-release buckles on the aqualung harness and jettisoning it. Bring the victim's arms through the center of the float and over the sides, in the latter case. Then remove the victim's mask and clear his mouth as prescribed above. Pinch his nostrils closed, place your mouth over his, and breathe into it as you would with the snorkel.

METHODS OF ARTIFICIAL RESPIRATION

Photos by Bob Ritta

Clear victim's lungs and air passages of water by lifting him by the midriff and shaking him.

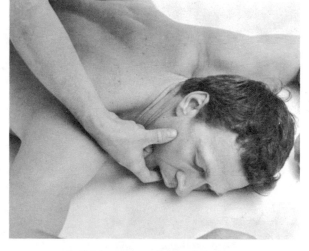

Pull his tongue forward before starting artificial respiration.

MOUTH-TO-MOUTH RESUSCITATION

This method is very effective and can be performed almost anywhere and in any position. It is especially valuable in cases of chest injury.

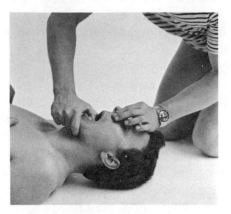

Hold victim's jaw in "jutting out" position with one hand.

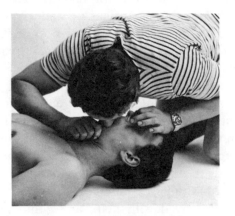

Place your mouth over his, making good seal. For inflation, breathe into victim with smooth, steady action until definite expansion of chest is noted. For deflation, remove mouth and allow victim to exhale. If he fails to do so, apply gentle pressure to chest.

BACK-PRESSURE, ARM-LIFT RESPIRATION

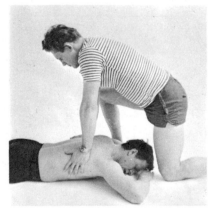

Kneel at head of victim. Place hands on the victim's back, as shown, keeping your arms straight and nearly vertical. Press slowly and firmly.

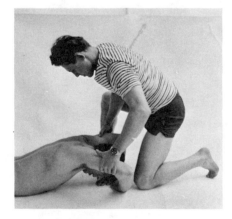

Release the pressure, and, leaning back, raise the victim's arms enough to arch his back and partly raise his chest from the ground.

BEAR-HUG, ARM-LIFT METHOD

Highly effective where the victim cannot be placed flat. Can be used even in water, with flotation gear.

Sit behind victim, arms around chest under his arms. Squeeze chest with both arms.

Raise both arms. Do everything possible to prevent obstruction; keep victim's tongue forward.

HIP-ROLL, BACK-PRESSURE METHOD

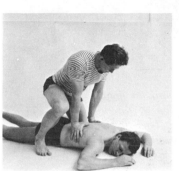

An excellent method, not too tiring if properly done. Especially valuable in cramped space or if victim's arms are injured.

Face victim's head. Kneel on one knee, well forward of victim's hip and with knee close in to operator's forearm. Grip hipbones with both hands.

CHEST-PRESSURE, ARM-LIFT METHOD

Effective. Usable in very cramped space, this method permits facing victim.

Seat victim; kneel straddling his legs. Grasp both wrists.

Raise victim's arms over his head. Be careful to prevent obstruction.

SCHAEFFER METHOD

An old stand-by, now outmoded.

There will be few situations where one of these methods cannot be used, but remember that almost any procedure that involves squeezing the chest or abdomen will move some air and is worth trying if nothing better can be done.

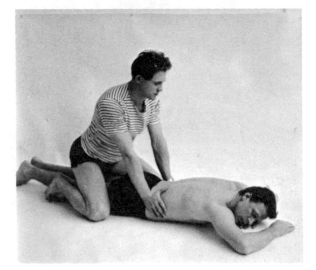

Straddle victim's thighs and place hands over lower ribs.

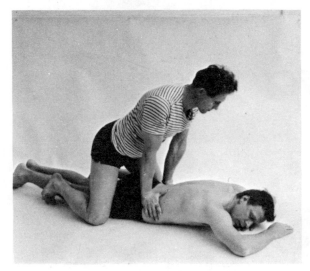

Lean forward on hands, keeping elbows stiff, to induce exhalation. Then lean back to allow inhalation. Continue, to breathing rhythm.

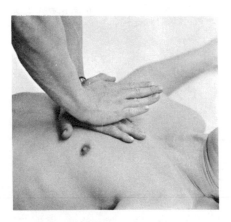

A sharp blow on the chest can revitalize an arrested heart.

EARDRUM RUPTURE

Ear squeeze and possibly eardrum rupture can result from not equalizing the pressure in your ears as you dive, from diving with a cold (blocked Eustachian tube), from external dry-suit squeeze, or from using earplugs.

SYMPTOMS:

> severe pain on descent as rupture occurs
> dizziness and nausea as cold water enters middle ear
> temporary disorientation
> loss of hearing in affected ear

SIGNS (depending on extent of damage):

> redness and swelling of eardrum
> bleeding into middle ear or outer ear canal
> spitting up blood
> blood blisters around eardrum

TREATMENT:

Hands off! If eardrum rupture is suspected, do not allow anything, whether water, instruments, or medications, to enter the ear. Close the outer passage with a bit of cotton and see a doctor as soon as possible to avoid possible infection. Rupture will heal in from two weeks to a month.

EAR INFECTIONS

Divers operating in tropical waters are peculiarly susceptible to external ear infections, especially by so-called fungus. While not especially dangerous if treated properly, infections can be very uncomfortable and sometimes incapacitating.

SYMPTOMS:

> crusting of ear canal
> itching or pain in ears
> exudation of fluid from ear canal

SIGNS:

> heavy accumulations of "fungus growth"
> dry flakes of same at external ear opening
> redness and swelling around ear canal

TREATMENT:

Preventive treatment is the best. Keep the ears always clean, dry, and clear of *excess* ear wax. Use drops of alcohol diluted in seventy percent of water to dry ears after each dive. Do not dive until healed. Look out for recurrences and see doctor if it persists.

ELECTROCUTION

Electrocution can result from careless handling of underwater electrical apparatus, such as electric cutting and welding torches and photographic lighting equipment. All electrical apparatus used in diving should be perfectly insulated and in perfect condition. To be on the safe side, in handling such equipment you must insulate yourself as well as the equipment.

SIGNS:

> unconsciousness
> cessation of breathing
> heart failure
> victim may have been unable to pull away from source of shock

TREATMENT:

Cut the electric current immediately and do not touch victim before doing so. Bring victim to surface and treat for heart failure (page 145). Give artificial respiration until victim is revived or pronounced dead (see "Drowning," page 136). Get medical assistance at once if possible. Keep victim at bed rest for at least twenty-four hours after he revives.

EMBOLISM (see "Air embolism," page 129).

EMPHYSEMA (see "Air embolism," page 129).

FACE-MASK SQUEEZE (see "Squeeze," page 149).

FAINTING

Fainting (syncope) is caused by a temporary failure in the body's automatic blood-pressure control system, which provides oxygen to the brain tissue. This failure, in turn, is caused by some acute stress, pain, or emotion. Unless it is accompanied by shock due to injury or loss of blood, it is not serious and the victim usually recovers in a minute or two.

SYMPTOMS:

 dizziness
 weakness
 nausea
 pallid or green color
 staggering
 collapse and unconsciousness

TREATMENT:

Fainting can often be avoided if, at the first symptoms, the victim either lies down with his head back and legs elevated, or sits down and leans over, placing his head between his knees. This allows oxygen-carrying blood to reach the vital brain tissue more readily. A fainting victim should be stretched out with legs elevated and head back until revived and rested. If he fails to revive within a few minutes, seek medical help immediately, for that indicates the presence of a more serious ailment. If the victim stops breathing, artificial respiration should be applied at once (page 136).

FISH POISONING

Internal fish poisoning. Certain species of fish are congenitally poisonous to eat and should be avoided as food at all times. These include porcupine fish and sunfish.

Fish meat that has become old, rotten, or rancid can also induce internal poisoning.

In addition, certain fish around some tropical coral reefs become poisonous to eat during brief periods of the year because of a mysterious disease called ciguatera. This disease is undoubtedly caused by some seasonal environmental food—probably a blue-green alga—which has not yet been isolated, and it can affect even prized table fish such as grouper and snapper, as well as other reef fish like barracuda, squirrelfish, parrot fish, jacks. Although there are as many methods of detecting fish infected with ciguatera as there are areas where it occurs, most are products of folklore rather than medical science and should not be relied upon. Dr. John Randall, a marine biologist with the University of Miami, is currently investigating ciguatera, and his reports to the International Oceanographic Foundation at that university should be followed. Meanwhile, you will have to take your chances when spearfishing in areas known to be affected by ciguatera, or test suspected fish by feeding samples to an animal and observing its reaction. The disease usually is not serious, but it can cause discomfort and even death.

SYMPTOMS (one to ten hours after eating fish):

 stomach cramps
 nausea and weakness
 vomiting
 diarrhea
 prolonged numbness and tingling sensation
 lack of coordination
 difficulty in breathing
 confused senses
 relapses on eating fish

TREATMENT:

> purge stomach as soon as symptoms appear
> try antihistamine
> avoid eating fish

External fish poisoning. Certain fishes are equipped with venomous spines poisonous to touch and should be avoided. These include stonefish, scorpion fish, stingrays, zebra fish, horned sharks, catfish, weaverfish, ratfish, toadfish, surgeonfish, and rabbitfish.

Almost all species of the jellyfish family are equipped with long, streaming tentacles containing thousands of tiny cells of venom, which cause severe acid stings.

Finally, the bite of some marine creatures, such as the octopus and the sea snake, can be very poisonous.

1. *Fish with poisonous spines* are lethargic and do not tend to scare off easily. Many camouflage themselves against the bottom and are difficult to detect, but a few are very colorful—black and orange being the predominant colors. Almost all favor tropical waters, and local authorities should be consulted for information concerning them before you dive.

SYMPTOMS:

> local pain within a few minutes
> reddening and inflammation of affected area
> hot, burning sensation
> dizziness, possible shock and fainting
> weakness

SIGNS:

> puncture wound
> local swelling and inflammation
> in stingray wounds, a spiny sheath may be left in wound

TREATMENT:

Get the victim out of the water as quickly as possible and put him at rest. Remove all foreign matter from the wound and wash thoroughly with antiseptic or clean, fresh water. If severe, encourage local bleeding by applying tourniquet—making small incisions and applying *mechanical* suction. Follow by soaking, preferably in hot or icy fresh water, remembering to loosen tourniquet for five minutes every thirty minutes. When pain has subsided, cover the wound and elevate the affected limb. Watch for signs of shock. If the wound is in the chest or abdomen, seek medical help immediately, for the victim's heart action may be affected.

2. *Jellyfish* are found in all waters of the world. There are 2500 known species, some dangerous and some not. The two most dangerous types—the Portuguese man-of-war, whose venom is said to be on a par with that of a cobra, and the sea wasp—favor tropical waters, the latter being found almost exclusively around northern Australia, the Philippines, and the Indian Ocean. Most jellyfish are small, their bodies seldom exceeding six inches in diameter, but their stinging tentacles may reach fifty feet. Avoid contact at all times—even when they are found "dead" on the beach. Wear protective clothing in infected waters.

SYMPTOMS (depending on species and extent and site of sting):

> from a mild prickly or stinging sensation to intense burning, throbbing, or shooting pain, which may render a victim unconscious
> stomach cramps
> numbness
> nausea
> backache
> loss of speech and frothing at the mouth
> constriction of throat
> difficult breathing
> sweating
> paralysis
> delirium
> convulsions
> shock

SIGNS:

> reddening and inflamation of affected area
> clinging pieces of almost transparent blue-green tentacles
> welts
> blisters
> swelling
> small skin hemorrhages

TREATMENT:

Get the victim out of the water and at rest quickly. Remove as many of the clinging tentacles as possible. Do not touch with hands; use gloves, cloth, seaweed, or even sand. Wash in fresh water. Apply weak ammonia or baking soda solution. If available, apply cortisone ointment, antihistamine cream, or anesthetic ointment. Otherwise try olive oil, sugar, cooling lotions, or ethyl alcohol, followed by cold compresses. Look out for shock (page 148).

3. *Poisonous bites* vary in severity according to their source. An octopus bite is not likely to occur or to be very serious if it does, although at least one cause of death has been reported as a result of one. Moray eel bites can be considered poisonous only in that they leave particles of slime and rotten matter in the wound that are conducive to infection. Sea snake bites are inflicted by small sets of fangs containing a potent venom, however, and should be treated as lethal snake bites. Octopuses are found in all waters, the moray eels in all tropical waters, and the sea snake in tropical coastal waters, especially in the Pacific and Indian Oceans. All should be avoided.

Octopus bites cause a stinging sensation, with swelling, redness, and fever around the affected area. There is no specific treatment, but severe cases may be treated as a poisonous spine wound.

Moray eel bites can cause severe lacerations, for they have needle-sharp teeth and a tenacious grip. Clean the wound thoroughly and apply antiseptic and dressing. If stitches are needed, see a doctor as soon as possible.

Sea snake bites have a delayed-action effect. There is no pain or reaction at the site of the wound itself, but after a delay of about twenty minutes to one hour, victims are likely to feel a general anxiety or else a general feeling of well-being. This may lead to thickening of the tongue, general muscular stiffness, and pain. Then other symptoms appear as follows:

SYMPTOMS:

> weakness, progressing to possible immobility
> drooping of eyelids
> tightening of jaw muscles as in lockjaw (tetanus)
> partial paralysis of throat area
> parched throat
> shock
> muscular spasms
> convulsions
> paralysis of face and eye muscles
> respiratory difficulty
> unconsciousness
> death (in twenty-five percent of cases)

SIGNS:

> local pain and reaction
> absence of pain after initial bite for at least twenty minutes
> two circular dots or two pairs of dots half an inch apart
> possibly a fang left in wound

TREATMENT:

Get victim out of water and at rest as soon as possible. Call Coast Guard or send for medical help. Apply tourniquet between wound and heart, remembering to loosen it for five minutes every thirty minutes. Promote local bleeding by making incision around wound and applying suction. Give antivenom treatment if possible. Treat for shock and get the victim to a hospital if at all possible. Try to capture snake for identification.

GAS PAINS (see "Stomach pains," page 150).

GAS POISONING

Unless a diver's air tank is mistakenly filled with some other gas than air, carbon monoxide is the only poisonous gas likely to be encountered in standard free-diving practice (see page 132). In all cases, exposure to fresh air and artificial respiration is the standard treatment.

HEART FAILURE (CARDIAC ARREST)

Electrocution, shock, and some respiratory accidents sometimes cause the heart to stop beating. When this happens, tissue anoxia (oxygen starvation) sets in rapidly and can cause irreparable brain damage in less than three minutes. Therefore, you cannot lose a second in treating heart-failure victims if permanent brain damage is to be avoided.

SYMPTOMS AND SIGNS:
unconsciousness
cessation of breathing
cyanosis (blueness)

TREATMENT:

Never assume that a victim is dead beyond recall. Sometimes, as Yandell Henderson, a physiologist, once said: "The engine is merely stalled and needs to be cranked." The first-aid practitioner can now give that vital "crank" to a victim, thanks to a revolutionary new closed-chest heart massage recently developed by Dr. William B. Kouwenhoven at Johns Hopkins Hospital, which can be used in conjunction with the mouth-to-mouth method of artificial respiration. All you need is quick judgment and two hands.

When heart failure is suspected, follow these simple steps as they were outlined in the pages of the *Reader's Digest:*

1. Check for pulse—the easiest place to detect it is not in the wrist but in the throat, on either side of the windpipe near the collarbone. If no pulse is apparent, start working at once. Don't waste seconds going for equipment or help. Try delivering a series of vigorous blows to the chest over the heart with your fist. If this does not work:

2. Lay the patient face up on a solid support, such as the floor; a bed or couch is too flexible.

3. Tilt the head far back. (If the head sags forward, the patient may become asphyxiated while you work.)

4. Kneel so that you can use your weight in applying pressure. Place the heel of your right hand on the breastbone, with fingers spread and raised so that pressure is only on the breastbone, not on the ribs.

5. Place your left hand on top of the right and press vertically downward, firmly enough to depress the breastbone one to one and a quarter inches. (With a child, use only one hand and relatively light pressure.) The chest of an adult, resistant when he is conscious, will be surprisingly flexible when he is unconscious.

6. Release the pressure immediately, lifting the hands slightly, then repeat in a cadence of sixty to eighty thrusts per minute, approximating the normal heart action.

7. The patient should be taken to the hospital as soon as possible. Even if apparently normal heartbeat and respiration have resumed, professional care will be needed.

8. Continue the massage until you get professional medical aid to take over, or right into the emergency room of the hospital. Continue too, if possible, the mouth-to-mouth breathing, until someone arrives with a tank of oxygen to take over. If you are on your own and the victim shows no response, continue with your efforts until rigor mortis sets in.

Medical men find it increasingly hard to say when a person is really dead beyond recall. Many of the old signs—like dilated eye pupils that won't contract under a bright light—are no longer considered valid. Thirteen years ago an eminent Cleveland surgeon set a heart to beating after seventy-five minutes of open-chest massage. Johns Hopkins doctors recently revived another after 105 minutes of closed-chest massage and administration of oxygen.

The astonishing new emergency treatment of heart failure has proved over seventy percent successful and is the greatest innovation in first-aid practice since the advent of mouth-to-mouth resuscitation.

HEAT EXHAUSTION

When working in extremely hot climates, it is necessary to wear protective clothing and increase your intake of fluids and salt to avoid heat prostration (exhaustion). Keep work to a minimum. Divers should never attempt to enter water at air temperatures over 90 degrees, for the same reason. Avoid exposure to intense heat when possible. Protect head with a hat and sun glasses. Once heat exhaustion occurs, the victim becomes more susceptible to recurrences.

SYMPTOMS:
>   dizziness
>   headache
>   restlessness
>   fast pulse
>   difficulty in breathing
>   faintness
>   weakness
>   collapse
>   continued sweating in spite of cold, clammy skin and internal fever
>   if suffering salt hunger, muscular twitching and cramps may occur

TREATMENT:

Lay the victim down in a cool, shady place and give weak solution of salt. Headache and exhaustion may linger. Seek medical help if victim fails to recover.

HEAT STROKE

Heat stroke is caused by extreme overheating of the body and can be avoided by tempering your activity and wearing protective clothing in hot environments. It is a very serious emergency, which requires immediate lowering of the body temperature if quick death or permanent brain damage is to be avoided.

SYMPTOMS AND SIGNS:
>   a sudden rise in body temperature
>   sudden collapse
>   skin extremely dry and hot
>   very rapid pulse

TREATMENT:

Do not lose a second. Immerse entire body in cold water, the colder the better. Apply iced compresses to head and neck. Give weak solution of salt when revived. Apply mouth-to-mouth artificial respiration if breathing stops. Seek medical help.

Divers, especially those on extended expeditions, suffer a variety of cuts, bruises, lacerations, blows, and other physical injuries. These must be anticipated by taking along a good first-aid kit, and a good knowledge of a book on first-aid practice such as the American Red Cross *First Aid Manual*. This chapter pertains only to accidents that result directly from diving.

JELLYFISH STINGS (see "External fish poisoning," page 143).

LUNG (THORACIC) SQUEEZE (see "Squeeze," page 149).

MEDIASTINAL EMPHYSEMA (see "Air embolism," page 129).

MORAY EEL BITES (see "External fish poisoning," page 143).

MOTION SICKNESS (see "Sea sickness," page 147).

MUSSEL CUTS (see "Barnacle and mussel cuts," page 132).

NITROGEN NARCOSIS

Nitrogen in air breathed under pressure at depths of one hundred feet or more has an intoxicating effect on the body similar to that of alcohol (page 47). Susceptibility and reaction vary from person to person and from day to day, but at depths beyond two hundred feet most divers are too "drunk" to operate effectively or safely. Narcosis can be avoided only by avoiding the depths at which it occurs (about 130 feet and more) and, to a degree, by mentally combating it with all your powers of concentration.

SYMPTOMS AND SIGNS:

    loss of judgment and skill
    a false feeling of well-being
    lack of concern for job or own safety
    common stupidity
    difficulty in doing even simple tasks
    peals of laughter at slightest provocation
    near unconsciousness at great depths

TREATMENT:

There is no treatment. The effects of nitrogen narcosis vanish rapidly with ascent into shallow waters. No traces remain by the time diver reaches surface.

OCTOPUS BITES (see "External fish poisoning," page 143).

OXYGEN DEFICIENCY (see "Anoxia," page 131).

PNEUMOTHORAX (see "Air embolism," page 129).

RAPTURE OF THE DEPTHS (see "Nitrogen narcosis," on this page).

SEA SICKNESS

Sea sickness can be a serious hazard to aqualung divers, for it can occur not only on the surface but underwater as well. Never attempt to dive a man if he feels the possible need to vomit. If the water is extremely rough, postpone diving operations until it calms down. Anyone who feels the need to vomit while participating in a dive should head for the surface immediately, for vomiting beneath the surface can cause strangulation and drowning.

SYMPTOMS:

    wooziness
    dizziness
    thick, dry tongue
    nausea
    vomiting

SIGNS:

    pallid or sickly green complexion
    thick speech
    lethargy
    nausea
    vomiting

TREATMENT:

Sea sickness is caused by a motion-induced upset of the balance mechanism in the inner ear. Several brands of motion-sickness tablets are available at most pharmacies without prescription. These will successfully prevent motion sickness in most cases, but they are of little help after motion sickness has set in, and they contain antihistamines, which render the victim too sleepy and careless to operate effectively during a dive. Unless a diver knows his reaction to motion-sickness tablets, he should try to avoid taking them before a dive.

Avoiding the thought of sea sickness and staying out on deck and deep-breathing fresh air tends to dampen the nauseous effects of sea sickness. Once the diver gets safely underwater, wave motion generally vanishes by the time he reaches the depth of fifty feet, and so do the adverse effects.

SEA SNAKE BITES (see "External fish poisoning," page 143).

SEA URCHINS

Sea urchins of various species are plentiful in all tropical and most temperate waters. Sea urchins are covered with long, needle-sharp spines, which easily penetrate the skin on even slight contact and usually break off. They cling to rocks, coral heads, and beaches. Often they are so numerous that swimmers can hardly avoid contact with them. A few species of the short-spined sea urchin are equipped with small, venom-carrying pincers which can be telescoped out through the spines for added protection.

Since the sharp, brittle spines can easily penetrate clothing, there is little protection against sea urchins except studiously avoiding them. When working at a fixed site, it is best to remove all the urchins from the area with a stick or spear before work begins.

SYMPTOMS:
    immediate intense, burning pain
    redness and swelling
    weakness
    possible faintness, numbness, and respiratory distress

SIGNS:
    black dots where spines broke off in skin
    redness and swelling of affected area sometimes white, pallid complexion
    possible faintness, numbness and respiratory distress

TREATMENT:

Remove as many of the broken-off spines as possible with tweezers or forceps, then cleanse, apply antiseptic, and cushion with a large, loose dressing. Leave those which are difficult to get at. Do not "pick around." Spines of most urchins will be dissolved and absorbed into the body within a few days. Others will leave long, lingering blue marks like a faded tattoo unless surgically removed by a doctor. If infection appears, seek medical advice.

The pincers of the venomous short-spined sea urchin remain active for several hours and should be removed immediately. The wound should then be treated as a venomous fish sting (see "External fish poisoning," page 143).

SHALLOW-WATER BLACKOUT (see "Anoxia," page 131).

SHARK ATTACKS

Shark bites usually appear in a rounded, half-moon shape matching the shape of the shark's jaws. Usually they are very sloppy wounds, with severe lacerations from the shark's many razor-sharp teeth. An entire section in the shape of the shark's jaw might be missing from the victim.

TREATMENT:

Get the victim out of the water immediately and stop the bleeding by placing a tourniquet between the wound and his heart. Remember to loosen it for five minutes every thirty minutes. Treat for shock (see "Shock," below) and seek medical help immediately by calling U. S. Coast Guard if required.

SHOCK

Shock results from a traumatic injury with loss of blood, severe burns, or any condition that results in loss of blood or body fluids. When shock occurs, the body cannot keep the blood pressure up, and tissues are starved for oxygen. Unless treated promptly and properly, it can result in death.

SYMPTOMS AND SIGNS:

    loss of blood or body fluid
    pulse very feeble and very rapid
    blue lips and fingernails
    cold sweat, paleness
    muscle spasms and shivering
    dizziness
    fainting and unconsciousness

TREATMENT:

Treatment of shock requires prompt medical attention. Stop bleeding by applying a tourniquet between wound and heart, remembering to loosen for five minutes every thirty minutes. Lay victim down, with head lowered and limbs elevated. Keep victim warm and reassured. Give stimulants but no alcohol. Victim urgently needs replacing of fluid loss with blood, plasma, or suitable substitute, and doctor should be notified of same. If conscious and not vomiting, mix one teaspoon of table salt and one-half teaspoon of baking soda in quart of water and give victim as much as he will take.

SKIN DISEASES (see "Dermatitis," page 135).

SQUEEZE

Squeeze (barotrauma) refers to any injury that comes about because of inability to equalize pressure between a closed air space in or on the body and outside water pressure (page 45). The free diver is subjected to a pressure squeeze on the ears, face mask, lungs, sinuses, and suit and is exposed to the following forms of pressure squeeze.

Ear squeeze (see "Eardrum rupture," page 141).

Face-mask squeeze is caused by failure to equalize the air pressure inside the standard face mask with the water pressure outside the mask during descent, with either snorkel or aqualung, by exhaling through nose. (It is im-

possible to equalize pressure in eye goggles, and they should be avoided.)

SYMPTOMS:

    sensation of suction around face and
      eyes
    pain

SIGNS:

    whites of eyes bright red from blood
    face swollen and bruised

TREATMENT:

Apply cold packs to bruised or bleeding areas. Give sedatives and pain-relieving drugs if required. Seek medical help for serious cases.

Lung (thoracic) squeeze can be caused by diving too deeply while holding breath with or without snorkel, by holding breath during descent, or by failure of air supply or demand regulator during descent. Usually, discomfort will cause the diver to surface before lung squeeze becomes severe.

SYMPTOMS:

    sensation of chest being squeezed dur-
      ing descent
    pain in chest
    difficult breathing after surfacing
    bloody, frothy sputum if severe

TREATMENT:

If severe, clear blood from mouth and place victim face down on slope so that drainage occurs. Give artificial respiration if breathing stops (page 136). Seek medical advice.

Sinus squeeze can be caused by blockage of opening leading from nose to sinuses. This occurs most often when diving while suffering head colds or other respiratory diseases. Avoid diving with head colds. Surface if sinus pain develops during descent.

SYMPTOMS:

    increasing pain in sinuses during de-
      scent
    pain relieved by ascent

SIGNS:
> blood and mucus discharge from nose
> in mask on ascent
> tender or painful sinuses

TREATMENT:

Avoid diving until cause subsides. Use nose drops, spray, or inhalator to open passages and promote drainage and passage of air. Seek medical advice if blood, pus, or other signs of infection appear in sinus discharge.

Suit squeeze is caused by compression of air spaces inside "dry type" exposure suits (page 25) by the increasing water pressure during descent. If the rubber seals over the outer ear canal, a rigid air space is formed there, and can cause external ear squeeze (page 44). Unless air is admitted into the dry suit to equalize inside pressure with outside pressure, continued descent will produce a tight, binding sensation that will press the folds into the skin.

SYMPTOMS:
> pinching of skin under folds of suit
> possible symptoms of external ear
> squeeze

SIGNS:
> red welts where suit folds were squeezed
> possible blood blisters and bleeding,
> usually around joints
> possible signs of external ear squeeze

TREATMENT:

Welts and bruises usually heal in time. Cold compresses will relieve blood blisters and bleeding. When squeeze develops, snort air into hood of suit through mask, or otherwise provide for entry of air into suit during descent. If ears are affected, treat for external ear squeeze (pages 44 and 141).

STOMACH PAINS

If a diver swallows air under pressure into his stomach or intestines during a dive, it ex-pands on ascent and the excess gas will have to be expelled. This is usually accomplished by Mother Nature, but if the gas is trapped in the middle of the intestine in a pocket it may cause stomach or intestinal pain.

SYMPTOMS:
> if mild, abdominal fullness
> if moderate, abdominal pain and
> cramps
> if severe, great pain and fainting

TREATMENT:

Stop ascent when intestinal pain is noted. Redescend until pain is relieved, then attempt to belch or break wind, but be careful not to swallow more air in attempting to belch. Resume ascent slowly and cautiously. Avoid swallowing air during dive, and don't chew gum during dive, or dive with badly upset stomach.

STRANGULATION

Strangulation is asphyxia (page 131) caused by obstruction of the body's air passages. Inhalation of foreign material such as chewing gum, false teeth, or vomit is the most likely cause of strangulation in free diving. The diver may have spasms of the larynx due to inhalation of water. It may be a complication of drowning, anoxia, or carbon dioxide excess, or other conditions that might require artificial respiration. Remove false teeth and do not chew gum or other things during a dive.

SYMPTOMS AND SIGNS:
> extremely difficult breathing
> noisy breathing, choking, gasping
> unconsciousness if severe or prolonged
> struggle to breathe eventually ceases

TREATMENT:

Remove obstruction if possible. Encourage victim to cough; pound him on back, turn him upside down. If nothing else works, you

ergency tracheotomy,
he middle of the tra-
v the larynx (voice
ade in the midline of
two fingers' breadth
dam's apple. At least
the windpipe must be
satisfactory opening,
e held open. The cut
a penknife, ice pick,
of doing harm in the
en compared to the
strangulation is not

ed, give artificial res-
to the hole.

SUBCUTANEOUS EMPHYSEMA (see "Air embolism," page 129).

SUIT SQUEEZE (see page 150).

SUNBURN

A bad sunburn can be not only an uncomfortable disease but an incapacitating one. It can ruin a diving trip very easily and inspire brilliant hindsight on the part of the victim. The real need is for foresight, however. Gradual exposure to the sun can be accomplished by sensible use of clothing and protective suntan creams, oils, and lotions. The neck and face are especially sensitive in men who have not built up their tolerance gradually. Remember that reflected sunlight is just as potent as direct sun rays and that it can occur on a hazy, overcast day as well as a sunny day, because ultraviolet rays are not filtered out by clouds. Men at sea should always protect their heads and eyes from the heat and glare of the sun by wearing a hat and sunglasses.

SYMPTOMS:
fever
pain
dizziness
possible prostration

SIGNS:
extreme redness
fever blisters

TREATMENT:

Treat sunburn as any other superficial burn. Use burn ointment or lotions. Bandages soaked with tannic acid (tea), vinegar, and boric acid are also good.

Do not pop blisters or peel skin with fingers, and avoid exposure to sun until skin temperature returns to normal.

SYNCOPE (see "Fainting," page 142).

THORACIC (LUNG) SQUEEZE (see page 149).

TRACHEOTOMY, EMERGENCY (see "Strangulation," page 150).

UNCONSCIOUSNESS
Here is the U. S. Navy treatment table for unconscious divers:

LOSS OF CONSCIOUSNESS DURING OR WITHIN 24 HOURS AFTER A DIVE

1. *If not breathing,* start manual artificial respiration at once. (See page 136.)
2. *Recompress promptly* if need is suspected even slightly. Call U. S. Coast Guard for transportation to nearest recompression chamber.
3. Examine for injuries and other abnormalities; apply first aid and other measures as required. (Secure the help of a medical doctor as soon as possible.)

Artificial respiration
(a) Shift to a mechanical resuscitator if one is available and working properly, but never wait for it. Always start a manual method first.

(b) Continue artificial respiration by some method without interruption until normal breathing resumes or victim is pronounced dead. Continue on way to chamber and during recompression. (Do not use oxygen deeper than sixty feet in chamber.)

Recompression

(c) Remember that an unconscious diver may have air embolism or serious decompression sickness even though some other accident *seems* to explain his condition.

(d) Recompress *unless:*

    (1) Victim regains consciousness and is free of nervous-system symptoms before recompression can be started.

    (2) Possibility of air embolism or decompression sickness can be ruled out without question.

    (3) Another life-saving measure is absolutely required and makes recompression impossible.

(e) Try to reach a recompression chamber, no matter how far it is.

(f) Treat according to tables on pages 123 and 124, depending on response. Remember that early recovery under pressure never rules out the need for adequate treatment.

VENOMOUS FISH (see "Fish poisoning," pages 142 and 143).

Chapter 10

UNDERWATER PHOTOGRAPHY

When skin diving first became popular, the greatest attraction seemed to be spearfishing. The number of poor helpless fish you could skewer in one dive session became the measure of how good a diver you were. Consequently, any living thing that had the misfortune to cross a diver's path usually wound up on his spear. Underwater life soon became scarce around the more popular diving areas. Heaps of fish were left to rot on the beach, incurring the wrath of bathers and conservationists alike. The predictable result was that divers acquired a bad reputation and skin diving soon became outlawed in many areas.

Today the situation has changed. Most divers who once got their kicks from the wanton killing of fish have discovered that it is much more gratifying and challenging to shoot fish with a camera instead of a spear gun. Consequently the underwater camera has replaced the spear gun as the diver's primary tool and the popular attitude toward skin divers has vastly improved. In fact, many conservationists and water sportsmen use the findings of underwater photographers to their advantage. Thus skin diving for underwater photography has come to be accepted as a constructive and interesting use of the privilege of exploring the last frontier left on earth. With the new breed of marine scientists, the diver must share the responsibility of preserving the wonders of the underwater world as best he can. Underwater photography reveals the wonders of the deep for others to enjoy vicariously as well. It's a game everybody wins —even the fish!

Special Requirements

If you are already a competent diver, all you need in order to take good underwater pictures is a basic knowledge of photography, some film, and a watertight camera or camera housing.

If you do not already have it, a basic knowledge of photography can be acquired by reading a good book on the subject and then practicing what you learned by shooting a few rolls of film on land. Once you discover what you must and must not do to get good pictures on land, it is an easy matter to get reasonably good pictures in clear water. Of all the special requirements of underwater photography, clear clean water is by far the most important. The camera is not so adaptable as your eye. If the water in which you plan to shoot is so dirty or full of suspended matter that everything seems blurred, that's the way it will look on film, and there is nothing you can do about it!

Underwater Cameras

If you already own a camera, the chances are that it will work just as well underwater as it does on land. All you need is an absolutely watertight housing to protect it against highly corrosive salt water. It's easy to construct a makeshift underwater housing for your camera by enclosing it in a heavy plastic bag sealed around an ordinary face mask by the metal clamp that holds the faceplate in place. However, flexible plastic is easily torn or punctured, and if you value your camera at all, I do not recommend this procedure. There are available a number of so-called "universal camera housings" made of rigid quarter-inch plastic or cast aluminum that accept a variety of cameras. The best of these are the Mako and the Bamboo Reef universal housings. Most of them can be rented at nominal fees from your local dive shop, and you should rent before you actually invest in a housing of any kind. When you are ready to buy a housing for your camera, I recommend the cast-aluminum variety over the plastic models simply because of their sturdier construction. You will probably be able to find a housing that is custom-made for your particular camera, ranging in price from $50.00 to $300.00, depending on the kind of camera you have.

If you do not already own a camera and you want to buy one with underwater photography in mind, I strongly suggest that you consider the new amphibious cameras. There are two cameras on the market today made to operate underwater as well as on land without special housings.

For the beginner or the budget-minded, the Mako Shark is ideal. Developed by photographer Jordon Klein, it is a simple, economical 2¼ × 2¼″ box-type flash camera made of styrene plastic that is good for depths to one hundred feet.

For the serious amateur or professional, however, the best bet is the new Nikonos amphibious camera made by the Nikon Camera Company of Japan. I watched the prototype of this revolutionary camera being developed by Captain Jacques-Yves Cousteau and Jean DeWouters aboard the M/V *Calypso* and can

Mako amphibious camera. Low-priced, self-contained unit excellent for beginners. Pressure tested to 100 feet. Takes 120 or 220 film that gives 12 or 24 exposures (2¼ × 2¼″) in color or black and white.

vouch for its remarkable versatility. Small enough to fit into your hand, the lens and mechanism of this 35mm camera are hermetically sealed with "O" rings within a metal body that can withstand pressures of depths

Photographer Chuck Irwin displays his Nikonos with flash. Notice his bulb holder, made of neoprene rubber.

Nikonos 28mm wide-angle lens.

to three hundred feet. A single lever triggers the shutter and advances the film and then locks for safety when not in use. The focus and aperture on the interchangeable wide-angle 35mm and 28mm lenses are easily adjusted and can be read in the dimmest light. The standard flash accessory is only adequate, but the flash socket works perfectly with other flash units as well as with strobe units. This makes for excellent color shots. Consequently, many top professional photographers rely almost exclusively on this small but mighty camera for their underwater work.

Nikonos amphibious camera. Ideal underwater camera that works equally well on land. Pressure tested to 300 feet. Needs no housing. 35mm film with rapid-fire film transport. Takes 35mm and 28mm wide-angle lenses plus underwater flash.

Movie Cameras

If you prefer motion picture to still photography, you can find plastic or cast-aluminum housings to fit most 8mm or 16mm movie cameras as well. Whether you shoot in 8mm (recommended for all amateurs) or 16mm (recommended for all professionals), I suggest that you use a camera with a battery-driven motor so that you can avoid having to stop and rewind the spring right in the middle of that once-in-a-lifetime shot. Although motor-driven cameras are readily available in the 8mm field, they are hard to come by in the 16mm category. Beautiful cast-aluminum housings are custom-made especially for the 16mm Bolex, Bell and Howell, and Kodak K-100 cameras. Beautiful battery-driven motors are also made for them. But none of the housings will accept the motors! All of them must be spring wound. The K-100 has the longest wind (forty feet) of these three most popular 16mm cameras.

Mako housing for 16mm or 35mm Arriflex motion-picture camera for professional work. Aluminum housing pressure-tested to 200 feet. Takes 400-foot magazine. 180° optical finder system.

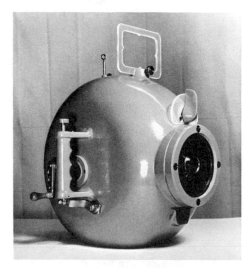

Jubamarine 16. This housing will accept most 16mm cameras, including electric motor and batteries.

Underwater housing for Rolleiflex camera. (Girl is Pat McKenney.)

Plexiglass housing can be homemade for most still or movie cameras. All-purpose controls may be purchased from most well-equipped diving-specialty shops. Cost of materials ranges from $10 to $100. Photo Dan Jones

Underwater Light Meters

An underwater light meter is indispensable to good underwater photography. The human eye is so adaptable to adverse light conditions that it can see many things that the camera cannot. Besides, different kinds of film require different exposures under given lighting conditions, and underwater lighting conditions are never the same from place to place, from depth to depth, or even from day to day. It is practically impossible to guess the proper exposure, regardless of how experienced you may be. Never trust your own judgment in determining underwater exposure settings. Always use a light meter.

If you already own a light meter, you can rig a makeshift underwater housing for it by placing it inside a strong Mason glass jar. The lid must be sturdy enough to withstand the pressure of the depths you expect to be working in or it will buckle and leak water. Round glass jars also cause slight errors in exposure readings due to the optical surface they create with the water. So, if you plan to shoot more than a few rolls of film underwater, it is best if you rent, purchase, or build a rigid plastic housing for your meter or purchase an amphibious meter that works equally well on land or underwater without a special housing. (I recommend the Sekonic Marine L-164, imported by Kanematsu New York, Inc., 1 Whitehall Street, New York City.)

Even if you have no exposure meter or no underwater housing for it, you can still get fairly good exposures by making a qualified guess as recommended below and then bracketing your shots—that is, taking one shot at the exposure you think best, then taking two more, one at one stop under that exposure and one at one stop over that exposure. This may

Author used Bolex and underwater housing to shoot his latest film, "The Sea in Your Future." Fast, low-grain color films, such as Eastman EF 16mm, have facilitated underwater moviemaking.

seem to be unnecessary extravagance to some, but the chances are that the film you expose will be the cheapest and most rewarding expenditure on your entire trip. You can make a fairly well-qualified guess at the proper exposure in the following manner.

Before you dive, look down into the water you are about to enter from several feet above it, and judge its clarity. If you can distinguish objects clearly on the bottom in fifteen or more feet of water, the clarity can be considered excellent. If you can distinguish form

but no detail, the clarity is good. If you can see only shadow, the clarity is only fair. If you can see nothing at all, don't bother to take your camera with you.

Having once evaluated the clarity, take a light meter exposure reading or use the film-data sheet provided in the package to determine what the proper exposure would be if you were shooting on the surface but in shadow. Then determine your underwater exposure by opening up one f-stop or the equivalent at the following depths according to the

Underwater photography permits you to record your thrills for posterity. Photo Mike Bunt

clarity of the water and then opening one f-stop for every ten feet of distance from camera to subject:

If the clarity is:	*Open one f-stop at:*						
Excellent	7 to 10′	25′	50′	100′	150′		
Good	1 to 10′	20′	35′	60′	85′	110′	
Fair	1 to 8′	15′	25′	40′	60′	80′	100′
Bad	Results dubious; try opening one f-stop every eight feet						

For example, if your surface exposure were 1/100 second at f/11, and you were ten feet down in water of excellent clarity, shooting your buddy who was ten feet away, you would open your aperture one f-stop for the depth and one more f-stop for the camera-to-subject distance. This would give you an exposure of 1/100 second at f/5.6.

Passing clouds and a windy, choppy surface will also affect exposures. A troubled sur-face will affect your judgment of the water conditions, and you must also stay alert for any light changes due to passing clouds ob-scuring the sun when you are submerged.

For crisp, clear pictures it is best not to attempt shooting when your subject is near the limits of your visibility. Remember, the closer the better. Make it a rule to keep your main subject within a third of the distance of your visibility.

Lenses, Films, and Processing

The type of lens you use plays a very im-portant role in the results of your underwater photography. Because of the suspended mat-ter in water, it is best to stay as close as pos-sible to your subject when shooting. Thus, the wider the angle lens you use, the closer you can get to your subject without sacrificing pic-ture content or quality. The wide-angle lens also gives you greater depth of field for better perspective and finer definition.

The type of film stock you use is another important consideration. Generally speaking, the faster the film speed, the heavier the grain of the emulsion and the fuzzier the resulting picture. Conversely, the slower the film speed, the finer the grain and the better the definition. This holds true for both color and black and white film. Thus, it is best to use the slowest, least grainy film that the light and clarity of the water will permit. Thus if you were shoot-ing black and white, I would suggest Pan-atomic-X or its equivalent at ASA 32 to 100. Otherwise, I would use the equivalent of Plus-X Pan at ASA 160 to 320 or Tri-X Pan at ASA 200 to 1200, in that order. If you were shooting color, I would suggest using the equivalent of Kodachrome II at ASA 25, Anscochrome or Ektachrome at ASA 32 or Ektachrome-X at ASA 64. Otherwise, I would use the equivalent of High Speed Ektachrome at ASA 160.

If you were shooting movies instead of stills, I would use Kodachrome II or its equivalent at ASA 25 if I intended to project the original. If I intended to pull copies for projection and keep the original intact, I would use the equivalent of Commercial Ektachrome at ASA 16 (with conversion filter in) or better yet the new Ektachrome EF at ASA 125 to 1200. The latter film is a revolutionary exception to the high-speed/high-grain problem, and I happily relied upon it in shooting my recent color feature, *The Sea in Your Future*. In spite of its high speed, it provides practically grain-free pictures with total color saturation plus high definition even when pushed far beyond its normal speed. Besides, its color is rather on the warm side and this compensates somewhat for the bluishness caused by the filtering effect water has on the color spectrum of light.

CAUTION: *If you shoot a film at a rated speed that is any higher than that recommended by the manufacturer, you must develop it accordingly or else notify your laboratory to do so.*

Color vs. Depth

The color spectrum of daylight comprises red, orange, yellow, green, blue, indigo, and violet. But water acts as a filter on the color spectrum of light. Consequently the color composition of light changes progressively with the depth. Just two inches beneath the surface, all the infrared rays of the color spectrum are absorbed and scattered by the water. Within twenty to thirty feet, all the reds have been filtered out. Orange is the next color to go. Then yellow vanishes and then, one by one, the other colors until from about one hundred feet only indigo and violet remain. This creates the blue-green cast characteristic of most waters. Blue and green are simply the only two colors that exist in deeper water depths, so everything appears to be blue-green. Even the surface of the sea appears to be blue-green (unless the water is so dirty that it transmits no light at all) for they are the only two colors that are reflected back into the sky.

Although color corrective filters may help in depths of less than twenty feet, the only sure way to reveal the true colors that exist underwater (but that are invisible to the human eye) is to restore the entire color spectrum of light with artificial illumination. This can be done by using flashbulbs, strobe lights, or underwater photoflood lights as close to the subject as possible.